CULTURAL /\RCHITECTS

THE Family LEGACY

Shaping Culture from the Inside Out

D1709852

WORKBOOK

CULTURAL ⋀RCHITECTS

OTHER RESOURCES BY THE AUTHOR

The Family Legacy- Shaping Culture from the Inside Out –
Best-selling book available on www.Amazon.com

The Cultural Architects Journal book- Your journey of faith and
character in shaping culture from the inside out. available on
www.amazon.com

The Family Legacy Subscription- www.culturalarchitects.org

Family Legacy Coaching- www.culturalarchitects.org

Family Legacy Conference- www.culturalarchitects.org

Family Legacy School- www.culturalarchitects.org

Family Legacy Encounter- www.culturalarchitects.org

Family Legacy Coach Approach to Family Workshop and other
Family Legacy E-Courses- www.culturalarchitects.org

Family Legacy Pastor and Small Group Leader Training-
www.culturalarchitects.org

Invite Randy and Lesli to Speak- www.culturalarchitects.org

THE Family LEGACY

Shaping Culture from the Inside Out

How to lead your family, live your legacy,
and shape culture in the process.

RANDALL W. BIXBY

CULTURAL ARCHITECTS

Published by **Cultural Architects** Publishing, West Des Moines, IA.

ISBN: 979-8610854540

This publication is designed to provide accurate and authoritative information with regard to the subject matter covered. It is sold with the understanding that the publisher is not engaged in rendering legal, accounting, or other professional advice. If legal advice or other expert assistance is required, the services of a competent professional should be sought.

For more information, please write:
Cultural Architects Publishing:

PO Box 65096
West Des Moines, IA. 50265
or call 1(515-229-3067)

Visit us online at _www.culturalarchitects.org_
Cover designed by Greg L. Roberts

CULTURAL ARCHITECTS

TABLE OF CONTENTS

CULTURAL ARCHITECTS

CULTURAL /\RCHITECTS

How to get the Most out of Your Family Legacy Journey and this Workbook.

First, take the Family Legacy Journey with other families in a small group. Second, choose to engage in Emotional Intelligence and the Coach Approach.

Emotional Intelligence,
How you show up in this family legacy work matters…This can be a horrible experience… or… this can be glorious experience! It is up to you which.

There is no greater opportunity to leave a lasting imprint on your family. How they experience you in this journey sets a lens of how they will remember and experience you in time moving forward. What a huge opportunity for good and bad, healing and wounding, joy and sorrow, acceptance and rejection. There's a lot at stake.

One of the key distinctions of The Family Legacy Model™ is *integrating the practice of emotional intelligence into the family context.* Self-governing our emotions and understanding the thinking that is driving them is essential for the success of any relationship. All relationships are improved with the practice of EQ. Whether in business, church, government, family, or in school the benefits of EQ are proven and measurable scientifically.

Here is how you and your family can get the most out of working the protocols on the Family Legacy Journey. Talk through this ahead of time and do a self-assessment regularly if you want the most out of this journey.

Be Kind	Don't be rude
Be Humble	Don't be proud
Be Empathetic	Don't be selfish
Be Teachable (open)	Don't be unteachable (closed)
Be Loving	Don't be hateful
Be Vulnerable	Don't be defensive
Be understanding	Don't be harsh
Be Intentional	Don't be lazy
Be Responsible	Don't be blaming
Be Consistent	Don't be inconsistent
Be Authentic	Don't be fake

CULTURAL ARCHITECTS

Be Forgiving	Don't be bitter
Be Supportive	Don't be critical
Be Engaged	Don't be detached
Be Safe	Don't be unsafe
Be Courageous	Don't be fearful
Be Truthful	Don't be deceitful
Be FUN	Don't be glum
Be a good Listener	Don't be all talk
Be Present	Don't be
Be Aware…	distracted Don't
	be apathetic

Your chances for success in every aspect of life increase dramatically if you choose to show up powerfully by practicing emotional intelligence. Just think how your family would thrive if all of the family members and participants agree to show up as outlined above. You can do it! You aren't alone.

The Coach Approach

Another key distinction of the Family Legacy Model™ *is integrating The Coach Approach into the context of the family.* The dynamic of family relationships are transformed when we intentionally partner with family members in a proven practice that supports one another in discovery, growth, and success. Imagine experiencing your family as a primary place of resource in your growth and success. For many, this is beyond their ability to imagine. For others, the concept is familiar, but the step by step process in unclear.

Coaching is one of the most empowering and invigorating modalities in creating growth and success offered today. To integrate this into the Family Legacy Model™ by investing into the personal growth and development of each member is a powerful way to do family. Family coaching is an effective way to build legacy while training our children how to bring coaching into their generations to come.

If you want to ensure the best outcome as you apply the Family Legacy Model™, you simply must understand how to facilitate supportive family coaching conversations effectively.

As you plan for the coaching conversations specifically designed in the protocols along with having coaching conversations in everyday life informally, you may want to review this section to keep your skills sharp. In addition, I have a digital E-Course on the Website entitled The Coach Approach to Family that will equip you in a detailed manner in learning a coach approach.

How about this? If you find yourself having a difficult time with any of the protocols or with managing yourself in the execution of them reach out for help. Contact our office. Talk with a Family Legacy Coach or Facilitator who is there to help you through it.

We have a number of ways to assist you with your Family Legacy Journey. You can attend one of our workshops that will better equip you to do the work at home. Our facilitators can even be brought into your home either by phone, online or in person to either coach you through or actually take your family through the protocols.

There are several online E-Courses, weekly webinars, video archives and a monthly membership subscription that give you access to tools and content to further support you in the successful execution of the protocols.

Above all, take action now, don't quit, and reach out for help in you need it! Blessings to you as you lead your family, live your legacy, and shape culture in the process!

IMPORTANT NOTE

While this work is unapologetcially based on a biblical worldview, we recognize that not all family units consist of a traditional mom, dad and kids. We reference choosing a 'leader' for these exercises and often refer to (mom or dad). The leader in your 'family' could be a grandparent or any other member with authority in the household. We recongnize many families are already split by divorce so this may be either/or mom/dad or step parents. Your 'family' may be a group of orphaned adults who have chosen to 'do life' together as a family. These principals are eternal and true and there is grace for any/all family dynamics.

CULTURAL /\RCHITECTS

THE FAMILY
REFORMATION PROJECT

Family Legacy EQ
(Emotional Intelligence) Protocol 1

The purpose of The Family Legacy EQ (Emotional Intelligence) Protocol™ is to create a family environment of safety, trust, support, forgiveness, love, purpose and FUN! The work a family does in this space will profoundly impact the family experience presently and the trajectory of the family line for future generations to come.

> *"Wise people are builders-They build families, businesses, communities....And through **intelligence** and **insight** their enterprises are established and endure."*
> *Pr. 24:3 TPT*

It takes **intelligence** and **insight** to establish a ***family legacy that wIll endure***. More specifically, it takes **emotional intelligence** and **relational insight** to avoid identity drift, to self-govern well, and steward the family as designed.

The Family Legacy EQ (Emotional Intelligence) Protocol™ is a set of exercises that equip families with a process to create an environment of safety, trust, support, forgiveness, love, purpose and FUN for their family! As a family discovers the emotional intelligence and relational insight these exercises deliver, they are empowered to love one another authentically. They are taught to use EQ tools for healthy communication, conflict resolution, self-awareness, personal responsibility, and so much more. The skills learned can be applied to every aspect of life and provide our children with valuable tools for success in life and leadership.

The core experiential exercises for the Family Legacy EQ Protocol™ below are transformative. They are designed to produce deep and lasting change to the way we self-govern and steward the family. You may want to review The Inside-Out Transformation Solution and A Word About Cultural Architect sections in Chapter Two to understand exactly how and the science behind them.

In spending the last 10 years in this space, I have come to see the **framework** of emotional intelligence as these five key practices. Growing in the understanding of these five skills and your mastery of their use in your family, your career, and your relationships will transform your leadership, your results, and your life.

- Self-Awareness
- Personal Responsibility
- Sustained Action
- Empathy
- Trust

All nine EQ exercises are life changing experiences that have the ability to transform individuals and families from the inside out. They are Romans 12:2-3 in action. Follow them meticulously step by step to get the most from them.

Getting through the exercises is NOT A RACE! They take as long as they take. They could be completed in a day or two as we do within our workshops. They can also be done one at a time over several weeks, as well as anywhere in between. The important thing is to consistently work on them and complete them at the *beginning* of your Family Legacy Journey. You will lay a solid foundation to build on if you do. This protocol is first for that reason.

REMEMBER, we are here to help you if you find leading these exercises to be difficult. Contact our office and talk with one of our coaches, make arrangements for us to lead your family through the exercises, or attend one of our workshops. Don't skip the exercises. They are a critical piece to establishing a healthy environment vital to an enduring legacy.

CULTURAL ARCHITECTS

FAMILY LEGACY EQ PROTOCOL

Family Legacy-
Personal Investigator EQ Tool

THE FAMILY
REFORMATION PROJECT

The purpose of The Personal Investigator EQ Tool™ provide the reader with a process that empowers you to change your results by changing your thinking and agreements. This tool is an inside out EQ transformational tool. Age appropriate sensitivity.

The 5-part Personal Investigator Process
1. Look for clues
2. Revelation of belief systems (thinking) hidden in the sub conscious or the heart. Neuro science- 85% of our decisions are made below our awareness
3. Awareness of how that thinking is showing up across my life and taking personal responsibility for choosing the thinking
4. Analysis of the costs and benefits of the thinking to me and others
5. Choice and commitment of new thinking moving forward.

Personal investigators look for clues. This process starts with you discovering your own clues. Pay attention to your behavior and feelings. Especially behavior that is problematic and feelings that are negative. Investigate areas of your life that are painful, that are not the way you want them to be, where you feel stuck or fearful.

Step One:

List the Behaviors you are discovering:

List the feelings you are discovering:

What you are doing or not doing (behavior)? What are you feeling? Once you have this awareness, proceed through the following series of questions.

Step Two:

What is the thinking in my heart causing this behavior or feeling?

CULTURAL ARCHITECTS

Step Two: (Continued)
Take your time to look inside of your thinking and be honest with what you discover. Use the list below to help spark your awareness. Is the thinking underneath the behavior of avoiding conflict that conflict is painful, fearful, unsafe, or will escalate to harm? Then write it down. Keep drilling down deeper in your thinking until you reach a thought that is underneath all of the other thoughts.

Here is a list of some of the most common belief systems that self-sabotage our results.

Common Destructive Mindsets:

- "Can't trust anyone."
- "I have to figure it all out first."
- "I already know it all."
- "I'm right or I have to be right and in control to be safe."
- "I'm not enough."
- "My value is based on my performance."
- "It won't matter anyway."
- "I'm afraid to fail and if I do, I will be rejected."
- "I'm overwhelmed, confused and don't know what to do."
- "I'm afraid of what other people think about me."

Once you have identified a mindset or belief system driving your behavior and feelings, continue to the next step.

Step Three:

Where else in my life is this thinking showing up?

Look around your life and see if this way of thinking is affecting other areas as well. We take our thinking with us everywhere we go. You will likely find it everywhere.

Step Four:

What are the costs and benefits of this thinking?

Before you say, "There's no benefit to this problematic mindset." Keep looking. We choose to believe things because there is some pay off or benefit. Even if it is not having to be responsible or not having to work hard, or getting to blame others.

Step Five:

What is my commitment moving forward?

Clearly state a new belief system or mindset that you are choosing to agree with moving forward. The more agreement your new thinking has with Truth the more powerful the shift and the better results you can expect.

CULTURAL ARCHITECTS

THE FAMILY
REFORMATION PROJECT

FAMILY LEGACY EQ PROTOCOL

Family Legacy-
Social Covenant EQ Tool™

The purpose of The Family Legacy Social Covenant EQ Tool™ is to provide a process for everyone in the family to create a set of agreements and expectations to *govern* the family environment in the home. These agreements establish the *family culture* with everyone weighing in to ensure their buy in. This culture shaping exercise and tool establish guidelines for how everyone will show up in the day to day and for the Family Legacy journey. Thus, creating certainty, trust, value, personal responsibility, and empathy in your family culture.

Step One:

Select a leader (dad or mom) and then gather the family after a great meal in a relaxed environment. If your children are grown or the family is spread apart geographically, you may execute this tool over the phone or digitally by a video app such as Zoom. Doing this together and with everyone having a voice is critical to overall success.

Secure a flipchart or white board and markers so that everyone can see for best results. Read the following explanation to everyone: You may need to translate for young children so that they understand clearly.

"As a way for us to come together as a family and better understand each other, better meet each other's needs, and to just make for our family a safe, loving, fun, trusting, and supportive environment. I want to do a fun exercise with you. I need everyone to participate and to not hold back what you really think and what you really want. Everyone's voice matters! This exercise is called The Family Legacy Social Covenant" Read the purpose of the exercise written at the top of the page.

Step Two:

Take your marker and write at the top of the paper or whiteboard the following:
"Family Legacy Social Covenant"
Directly underneath that and starting at the left edge write the following four questions. Be sure to evenly space the four questions from top to bottom of the paper leaving equal space between each one to write responses. You can read these questions aloud as you write them.

Say, "We are going to work together to answer four questions that will make things awesome around here."

CULTURAL ARCHITECTS

1.) What do you want/need from me?

2.) What do I want/need from you?

3.) What do we want/need from each other?

4.) How will we resolve a broken covenant?

Step Three:

Go back to question one and invite everyone to answer the question what do you want from us? Write down and restate the answers that are given. Think especially about "how" your children want you as parents to show up. What kind of character qualities do they want from you? Specific tasks or requests are ok too but determine how they fit into a bigger picture. Write them all down. Ask for anything else from any one. Have them explain their thinking. Be sure to hear from everyone. _____

Examples:
Kindness, love, fun, keep agreements, read stories, help with homework, honesty, leadership, help with spiritual growth, advice for dating, later curfews, more $$ for allowance and so on.

When everyone has participated. Move on to the next question.

Step Four:

Go to question number two and begin sharing what you as parents want/need from the children. Be specific. Write down your responses. As in Step Three, think about how you want them to show up. What kind of character qualities do you want from them? Specific tasks or guidelines are appropriate here as well. _____

Examples:
Keep our agreements, be home on time, do your share of the chores, give your best in school, be authentic, be vulnerable, be truthful, be present, work hard, etc. Explain your thinking.

When you finish sharing, move on to the next question.

Step Five:

Go to question number three and invite everyone to answer the question what do we need/want from each other? Follow the same guidelines for the previous questions mentioned above. Write down the responses. Have everyone explain their thinking. Make sure you hear from everyone. _____
When everyone has finished sharing, move on to the final question.

CULTURAL ARCHITECTS

Step Six:

Go to question number four and invite everyone to answer the question How will we resolve a broken covenant? Say, "We are essentially determining the consequences and the process that we as a family will agree to follow when anyone fails to keep our Family Social Covenant agreements listed above." _____

Talk openly. What are the consequences? More importantly, answer this question in your discussion. "How will we get back into agreement?" The goal of this tool is to create and steward the environment that you have all agreed to. The environment that meets each other's wants and needs as agreed. _____

Don't be afraid to say what you need. Do not agree to anything that you aren't willing to keep. Change the agreement so that you all have an opportunity to "choose in" to the covenant.

Example:
The Biblical practice for restoring broken agreements is to first go one on one to the person and ask them why they are out of agreement and what will it take for them to get back into agreement. If that doesn't work, take another family member with you and revisit the same two questions. If that still doesn't work, it's time to go to the highest authority in the family and have them ask the same two questions.

The goal is to keep our agreement and steward the environment of our home responsibly by all members involved.

NOTE:
There may come a time to renegotiate the agreements as a family. Follow the same process and discuss the thinking underneath the requested changes. Keep working at it and massaging it until you can all come into agreement with the revision and lock in the changes.

Do this Together. Learn how everyone is responsible to create and steward the environment and the culture of the home.

By doing this exercise with the entire family, you are also teaching them how to use this tool in their lives and with generations to come.

Step Seven:

Have everyone express their agreement and buy in to the Family Legacy Social Covenant by having them sign their name to the flip chart or white board document. **Take a photo of it. Rewrite it into a document and pass it out.** Check-in on how the family is doing with the covenant at Family Rituals or regularly.

CULTURAL ᴀRCHITECTS

THE FAMILY
REFORMATION PROJECT

Family Legacy-
Healthy Communication
Empathetic Listening EQ Tool

The purpose of The Healthy Communication Empathetic Listening EQ Tool is to equip the family with a process to learn and grow the important communication skill of empathetic listening. To equip the family to listen for understanding beyond listening to respond. To set an expectation in the family that it is safe to speak, that everyone has a voice that needs to be heard, everyone matters. To eliminate misunderstandings, assumptions and judgements. All for the purpose of more deeply connecting with family members in an environment of honor, safety, trust, and love.

Reminder of what empathetic listening IS NOT!:

In brief, here are the six ways of automatic listening Toomey describes. They describe what empathetic listening IS NOT!

1. Agree/Disagree -   unending assessment
2. Personalizing   taking everything personal
3. Already know/fit   not clean slate
4. Safety   looking good at all costs
5. Accurate/inaccurate   describing or labeling
6. Resignation   won't matter any way

All of the above listening styles have one thing in common. The energy and conversation that is happening in the head of the listener in one way or another, is focused on *themselves* not the one who is speaking. They are allowing in just enough information from the speaker to empower their own thoughts and conversation with themselves about what they think about what is being said.

Reminder of what empathetic listening IS:

It is listening to fully understand the who, what, when, where, why, and how of the speaker. Empathetic listening starts here and then adds to that the emotions, facial expressions, body language, and tone of voice of the speaker.

All of this is done with a focus of energy on the speaker not on the listener for the purpose of fully understanding the experience of another human being.

Remember what empathy is, "Empathy is walking in another person's shoes with full understanding."   Garry Bixby

CULTURAL ARCHITECTS

Step One:

Select a leader (dad or mom) and then gather the family after a great meal in a relaxed environment. This exercise must be done in a face to face manner and not over video for best results. Have the leader read or share the purpose and reminders of what empathetic listening is and is not written above.

Step Two:

Instructions:

Leader says, "Let's practice empathetic listening through an experience. In a moment, we are going to pair off in groups of two." (Make sure children are paired with an older sibling or adult) "Each person will be asked to answer three questions. I'll let you know when to begin and when to stop talking. Each person will share for 4-5 minutes on each question while their partner practices empathetic listening. I will tell you when to switch and have the other partner practice listening."

Leader says, "Remember this is a listening exercise. Notice if you are listening from one of the automatic ways of listening or with empathetic listening. When you are listening, choose to not speak, keep eye contact, watch body language and facial expressions, and pay attention to the tone of voice." "Go ahead and choose a partner now. Determine which partner will go first in each pair. When you are settled, sit quietly and wait for the first question." "Please be open and honest in your responses."

Step Three:

Leader says, "Here is the first question partner one." *"What do you like or appreciate most about our family?"* (repeat the question) Leader says, "Partner two, you are practicing empathetic listening, partner one begin."

Watch the clock and gauge the participation. If family members are enthusiastically engaging, allow more time for responses. If not, say, "Partner one, stop talking." at the 4-minute mark.

Leader says, "Partner one, it's your turn to practice empathetic listening, partner two same question, *what do you like or appreciate most about our family? Partner two begin."*

Watch the clock and gauge the participation. If family members are enthusiastically engaging, allow more time for responses. If not, say, "Partner two, stop talking." at the 4-minute mark.

Step Four:

Leader says, "Here is the second question partner one." *"What do you dislike most about our family?"* (repeat the question) Leader says, "Partner two, you are practicing empathetic listening, partner one begin."

Watch the clock and gauge the participation. If family members are enthusiastically engaging, allow more time for responses. If not, say, "Partner one, stop talking." at the 4-minute mark.

Leader says, "Partner one, it's your turn to practice empathetic listening, partner two same question, *what do you dislike most about our family?* Partner two begin."

Watch the clock and gauge the participation. If family members are enthusiastically engaging, allow more time for responses. If not, say, "Partner two, stop talking." at the 4-minute mark.

Step Five:

Leader says, "Here is the third question partner one." "What do you wish was different in our family?" (repeat the question) Leader says, "Partner two, you are practicing empathetic listening, partner one begin."

Watch the clock and gauge the participation. If family members are enthusiastically engaging, allow more time for responses. If not, say, "Partner one, stop talking." at the 4-minute mark.

Leader says, "Partner one, it's your turn to practice empathetic listening, partner two same question, *what do you wish was different in our family?"* Partner two begin."

Watch the clock and gauge the participation. If family members are enthusiastically engaging, allow more time for responses. If not, say, "Partner two, stop talking." at the 4-minute mark.

Step Six:

Debrief and Learning:

Leader bring everyone back together and say, "Let's talk about what we learned by everyone joining me is a discussion that addresses a few key questions one at a time."

1. What did you learn about automatic listening?
2. What did you learn about empathetic listening?
3. How did it feel to listen and be listened to with empathetic listening?
4. What did we learn from the answers to the three questions?

Allow ample amount of time for everyone to respond to the discussion. Take notes.

Step Seven:

Application:

Leader says, "Given all that we have learned, how will we each apply these lessons specifically and practically in our day to day family life?" Allow each person to respond.

CULTURAL ARCHITECTS

THE FAMILY
REFORMATION PROJECT

FAMILY LEGACY EQ PROTOCOL

Family Legacy-
Healthy Communication
Speaking the Truth in Love EQ Tool

The purpose of The Healthy Communication Speaking the Truth in Love EQ Tool™ is to equip the family with a process to learn and grow in giving and receiving feedback in a healthy way. To avoid making assumptions about motives. To avoid misunderstandings and judgements. To ensure that family members receive the benefits of truth spoken in love instead of blame, accusation, sarcasm or criticism. To show the family how to take personal responsibility in both giving and receiving feedback. All of this keeps the family environment a safe and supportive one where family members help each other learn and grow.

Step One:

Select a leader (dad or mom) and then gather the family after a great meal in a relaxed environment. This exercise must be done in a face to face manner and not over video for best results. Have the leader read or share the purpose for the exercise written above.

Step Two:

Discussion:
Leader gathers everyone together and says, "I want us all to join in a discussion about how to speak the truth in love, or feedback by addressing a few key questions one at a time." Leader – draw out of people their responses and write up on a flipchart.

1. What is feedback?   (one person's opinion or experience of another person)
2. What is the value of giving good feedback?   (help another grow, learn, improve)
3. What is the value of receiving good feedback?   (I grow, learn, improve)

Step Three:

Discussion and Teaching:

Leader asks:
- "What is important for us to do when we give feedback to someone?"
  - Draw out answers from everyone and write up on a paper
  - Then cover the following points with the family
    - Speak the truth in love
    - Speak what you see (behavior)
    - Do not make assumptions of why or assign motives

Leader asks: (continued)
- Ask, "what was the thinking when you _____
- Ask for permission, "May I give you some feedback?"
- Don't criticize, berate, talk down at, or be rude
- Be kind

Leader asks:
- "What is important for us to do when we receive feedback from someone?"
  - Draw out answers from everyone and write up on a paper
  - Then cover the following points with the family
    Listen non-defensively
    Trust the people as being honest and well meaning
    Ask for clarification if necessary, "Help me understand…"
    Play detective on yourself during feedback… how am I feeling?
    How am I behaving? What am I thinking?
    Ask yourself, is there even a thread of truth to what this person is saying that I can own or take responsibility for?
    Ask yourself, how can I learn, grow, or change and improve?
    Don't take yourself too seriously. We can all grow. It's a good thing.

Step Four:

Instructions:
Leader says, "Let's practice speaking the truth in love by giving and receiving feedback through an experience. In a moment, we are going to pair off in groups of two." (Make sure children are paired with an older sibling or adult) "Each person will be asked to answer two questions, one at a time. I'll let you know when to begin and when to stop talking. Each person will share for 2-3 minutes on each question while their partner practices empathetic listening. After each answer the partner who was listening, will give 2-3 minutes of feedback to the partner who just finished answering a question. All feedback will come by using the phrase, "My experience of you is…" followed by a brief offering of feedback- speaking the truth in love." I will tell you when to switch and which partner is speaking and listening in the exercise.

Leader says, "Remember this is a giving and receiving feedback exercise. Notice how you are thinking and feeling as you are both giving and receiving feedback."

"Determine which partner will go first in each pair. When you are settled, sit quietly and wait for the first question." "Please be open and honest in your responses to the questions and in your giving of feedback."

CULTURAL ARCHITECTS

Step Five:

Question one to Partner One:
Leader says, "Here is the first question partner one." *"Describe a failure in your life and the lessons you learned as a result?"* (repeat the question) Leader says, "Partner two, you are practicing empathetic listening and preparing to give feedback in the form of "My experience of you is…" once I tell you to. Partner one begin."

Watch the clock and gauge the participation. If family members are enthusiastically engaging, allow more time for responses. If not, say, "Partner one, stop talking." at the 3-minute mark.

Leader says, "Partner two, it's your turn to give feedback to partner one's comments. You will use the phrase, "My experience of you is… over and over followed by your feedback. **Think about the guidelines mentioned above for how to give feedback.** Partner one, remain silent during the feedback. Partner two begin."

Watch the clock and say, "Partner two, stop talking." At the 3-minute mark.

Question two to Partner One:
Leader says, "Here is the second question partner one." *"What is one of your biggest fears and why?"* (repeat the question) Leader says, "Partner two, you are practicing empathetic listening and preparing to give feedback in the form of "My experience of you is…" once I tell you to. Partner one begin."

Watch the clock and gauge the participation. If family members are enthusiastically engaging, allow more time for responses. If not, say, "Partner one, stop talking." at the 3-minute mark.

Leader says, "Partner two, it's your turn to give feedback to partner one's comments. You will use the phrase, "My experience of you is… over and over followed by your feedback. **Think about the guidelines mentioned above for how to give feedback**. Partner one, remain silent during the feedback. Partner two begin." Watch the clock and say, "Partner two, stop talking." At the 3-minute mark.

Step Six:

Question one to Partner Two:
Leader says, "Here is the first question partner two." *"Describe a failure in your life and the lessons you learned as a result?"* (repeat the question) Leader says, "Partner one, you are practicing empathetic listening and preparing to give feedback in the form of "My experience of you is…" once I tell you to. Partner two begin."

Watch the clock and gauge the participation. If family members are enthusiastically engaging, allow more time for responses. If not, say, "Partner two, stop talking." at the 3-minute mark.

Question one to Partner Two: (continued)
Leader says, "Partner one, it's your turn to give feedback to partner two's comments. You will use the phrase, "My experience of you is… over and over followed by your feedback. **Think about the guidelines mentioned above for how to give feedback.** Partner two, remain silent during the feedback. Partner one begin." Watch the clock and say, "Partner two, stop talking." At the 3-minute mark.

Question two to Partner Two
Leader says, "Here is the second question partner two." *"What is one of your biggest fears and why?"* (repeat the question) Leader says, "Partner one, you are practicing empathetic listening and preparing to give feedback in the form of "My experience of you is…" once I tell you to. Partner two begin."

Watch the clock and gauge the participation. If family members are enthusiastically engaging, allow more time for responses. If not, say, "Partner two, stop talking." at the 3-minute mark.

Leader says, "Partner one, it's your turn to give feedback to partner two's comments. You will use the phrase, "My experience of you is… over and over followed by your feedback. **Think about the guidelines mentioned above for how to give feedback**. Partner two, remain silent during the feedback. Partner one begin." Watch the clock and say, "Partner two, stop talking." At the 3-minute mark.

Step Seven:

Debrief and Learning:
Leader bring everyone back together and say, "Let's talk about what we learned by everyone joining me is a discussion that addresses a few key questions one at a time."

1. What did you learn about giving feedback?
2. What did you learn about receiving feedback?
3. How did it feel to give and receive feedback using the guidelines?
4. How can you grow and improve or learn from the specific feedback?

Allow ample amount of time for everyone to respond to the discussion. **Take notes.**

Step Eight:

Application:
Leader says, "Given all that we have learned, how will we each apply these lessons specifically and practically in our day to day family life?" Allow each person to respond.

THE FAMILY
REFORMATION PROJECT

FAMILY LEGACY EQ PROTOCOL

Family Legacy-
The OOOH NO! EQ Tool

The purpose of the OOOH NO! EQ Tool™ is to equip the family with a process to let go of resentment and bitterness in order to avoid its self-destructive effects. To grow in love, forgiveness, conflict resolution, and problem solving within the family context. Unresolved conflict is a deadly blow to any relationship, especially in the family. This exercise will create a pathway for resolving offenses in order to create a loving, supportive, and safe environment at home.

Step One:

Select a leader (dad or mom) and then gather the family after a great meal in a relaxed environment. This exercise can be done in a face to face manner for best results, or over video app if need be. Have the leader read or share the purpose for the exercise written above.

Step Two:

Review:
Leader says, "Here are the three parts to the OOOH NO program (mindset) that runs so quickly while cloaked and almost invisible to our awareness." Write the three parts on a flipchart paper while reading them.

"**O**ffense - Any negative emotional response to something you *think* was said or done."
"**O**pposition: Putting up of a wall or breaking off of communication."
"**O**nslaught: The attempt to get even."

Leader says, "When this happens in the family people avoid each other, don't share openly and vulnerably with one another, and get in resistance to healthy flows of interaction with each other. They get on each other's nerves and annoy one another."

Leader says, "When this happens, there is a deep breakdown of the kind of healthy environment in the home required for healthy family interaction and the creation of a powerful family legacy."

CULTURAL ARCHITECTS

Step Three:

Instructions:
Leader says, "In a moment, we are going to each answer a set of questions individually **on a separate piece of paper** as we address the places in each of our lives where we knowingly or unknowingly find ourselves in the OOOH NO program. I will give you the questions, one at a time, and I want each of you to write down your responses as they come to you. We will process our answers together in a debrief once we have completed the process."

Step Four:

Questions:
Leader says, "Question number one, question, do you ever have a negative emotional response to a family member? Write down your negative emotional responses to your family member in the past 30 days as best as you can remember_____

Leader: take the appropriate amount of time to allow members to mindfully complete their answers to the question.

Leader says, "Question number two, question, describe where you have put up a wall, stop communicating with, or avoided a family member in the last 30 days because of a negative emotional response? Write down your responses on the paper." _____

Leader: take the appropriate amount of time to allow members to mindfully complete their answers to the question. (special consideration may be required for younger children)

Leader says, "Question number three, question, Have you ever attempted to get even? How? Write down your responses on the paper."_____

Leader: take the appropriate amount of time to allow members to mindfully complete their answers to the question (special consideration may be required for younger children)

Step Five:

Debrief and Learning:
Leader bring everyone back together and say, "Let's talk about what we learned by everyone joining me is a discussion that addresses a few key questions one at a time."

1. What did you learn about having negative emotional responses to family members? (allow for everyone to share their answers)
2. What did you learn about how you may have put up a wall or cut off communication? (allow for everyone to share their answers)

Debrief and Learning: (continued)

3. What did you learn about how you have attempted to get even? (allow for everyone to share their answers)
4. What will you commit to do moving forward to resolve the things that are not acceptable to you? (allow for everyone to make their commitments to the family)

Remember:

The remedy to this self-destructive belief system is to:

• engage in open, honest, responsible communication
• give a gift
• forgive and let go

Step Six:

Application:

Leader says, "Given all that we have learned, how will we each apply these lessons and remedies specifically in our day to day family life?" Allow each person to respond.

THE FAMILY
REFORMATION PROJECT

FAMILY LEGACY EQ PROTOCOL

Family Legacy-
Fact Story EQ Tool

The purpose of the Fact / Story EQ Tool™ is to equip the family with a process to self-govern their healthy choice of responses to whatever life has to throw at them. This elite EQ process will empower the family to find the good in any situation past, present or future and ensure the most valuable outcomes. This EQ exercise and tool will bring freedom to families from the lies that could ensnare them for decades. By self-governing their thinking, they can redefine their past, present, and future through active agreement with a good God and His wisdom. Romans 8:28 in action!

Step One:

Select a leader (dad or mom) and then gather the family after a great meal in a relaxed environment. This exercise can be done in a face to face manner for best results, or over video app if need be. Have the leader read or share the purpose for the exercise written above.

Step Two:

Review:
Leader says, "We live in several realms at the same time as human beings. We will address two of those realms in this exercise, the realm of *fact* and the realm of *story* or meaning. They are in fact, two separate realms. However, difficulty occurs when we start to combine these two together as if they are the same."

Leader says, "It is profoundly important to recognize that facts and stories are separate and not one-in-the-same. They only become one-in-the-same when a person chooses to connect a story to a fact. We each have been given the ability to choose what story or meaning we want to assign to any given fact."

Leader says, "Why is this important? Because healthy self-governing means that we are actively engaged in determining which story we will assign to life's facts that come our way. Actively choosing to agree with Truth and His meanings of a fact will bring life, freedom, peace, joy, and fruitfulness."

CULTURAL ARCHITECTS

Step Three:

Instructions:
Leader says, "In a moment, we are going to join together in answering some key questions and have a discussion over our answers. I will give you the questions, one at a time, and I want each of you to share your responses as they come to you. I will write down our responses up **on the flipchart paper** while we discuss them. Finally, I'll lead everyone through an exercise, and we will process the exercise together in a debrief once we have completed the process."

Step Four:

Questions:
Leader says, "Question number one, question, how would you define a **FACT**?" Leader writes the word "FACT" at the top left of the paper and then writes down the responses from family members. Use small size writing so that everyone can read it AND you can get a lot of answers written on the paper. Discuss and settle on a definition. Circle it.

Leader says, "Question number two, question, how would you define a **STORY**?" Leader writes the word "STORY" on the paper and then writes down the responses from family members. Use small size writing so that everyone can read it AND you can get a lot of answers written on the paper. Discuss and settle on a definition. Circle it.

Leader copies the illustration below on a second blank flipchart paper

Examples:

FACT | STORY
                 |
                 |
                 |
                 |
                 |
                 |

Leader says, "I'm going to write three facts in the fact column." and then says *while writing* in the fact column, "first born," and underneath that, "wears glasses," and underneath that "divorced."

Leader says, "Anyone here the first born? Anyone here wear glasses? Anyone here divorced or know someone that is divorced? Is that a fact or meaning? That's - a fact. It is something that happened in time and space and was measurable or observable."

Leader says, "What was the story you told yourself about it or the meaning you gave it? You gave it a story. What was it? What are some other potential stories for the facts?"

Step Four: continued
Leader (writes in the right column the various stories for each of the facts on the left)-
Make sure that you have more than one story or meaning for each fact.

Leader says, "As humans, we can't stand for things not to have meaning. So, we assign meanings or stories to the facts in our lives. Then we create new facts to justify the meaning we've given them. You'd have to do that, or you'd have a conflict of reality."

Leader says, "Because we each have the ability to choose any story for any fact and then we automatically gather more facts in life to confirm the story we pick, why is it so important which story we choose?"

Leader, draw out responses from everyone. Go up to the examples in your completed illustration above.

Leader says, "For example, why is it important to choose one story of what divorce means over a different story of what it means?" "Why does choosing the story that divorce is painful but leads to healing and a fresh start a better story than men are pigs or women are controlling or people can't be trusted?" draw out answers.

Leader drive home the point that whatever story we choose becomes how we will experience life going forward. Life happens from us not to us!

Leader says, "The stories we choose determine how we will experience life."

Step Five:

Exercise:
Leader hand out blank sheets of paper and pens. Have everyone draw a line from the top to the bottom of the paper in the center and write the word "FACT" on the top left side and write the word "STORY" on the top right side like illustrated below.

```
FACT              |        STORY
                  |
                  |
                  |
                  |
                  |
                  |
```

Instructions:
Leader says, "I want you to each think of one FACT that happened in your past that was very painful. Maybe an accident, injury, parents' divorce, rejection from a friend, bullying, broken promise, betrayal, or abuse. Just one thing that was emotional." "
"Now write that FACT at the top of the FACT column in a few words." *Give everyone 3-5 minutes to complete this.*

CULTURAL ARCHITECTS

Step Five: (continued)
Leader says, "Now I want you to write down the old story you choose to give that fact at the top of the STORY column on the right. What did you choose to make that fact mean about yourself? About God? About men or women? About how the world works?" *Give everyone 3-5 minutes to complete this.*

Exercise:
Leader says, "If… we have the power to choose what stories or meanings we give to the facts in our lives, and we do, then which meanings are going to do us and others the most good? Which ones will give us the greatest chance for love and acceptance? For abundance and destiny? For quality relationships and a culture shaping faith?"

Leader says, "Who really knows what is best for us and how to get the most good out of every situation? God does! Romans 8:28 says that "God will work all things together for good to those who love Him and are called according to His purpose…"

To come into agreement with God over what facts mean, demonstrating it consistently, is empowering! It can redefine your past, reframe your present, and create your future!"

New Story:
Leader says, "Since we have the power to choose our story, it's time to write a new STORY for that old painful FACT above. On your sheet of paper towards the lower half of the paper write the exact same FACT again that is at the top of your paper. Now, over on the right side of your paper under the old STORY, write your new STORY. Write down how God sees what happened in the FACT. Write down what he was doing, teaching, showing, healing, etc. in the FACT. Write a new story that agrees with how God wants to use for good what you experienced as bad. Go on and write it now."

Give everyone 5-10 minutes to complete their new STORY. You may need to help members make the shift to see the good and to redefine their story.

Step Six:
Debrief and Learning:
Leader bring everyone back together and say, "Let's talk about what we learned by everyone joining me is a discussion that addresses a few key questions one at a time."

1. What did you learn about facts and stories?
2. What did you learn about rewriting old stories?
3. How did it feel to rewrite the old into a new story?
4. What do you now know about writing good stories in real time as facts happen?

Allow ample amount of time for everyone to respond to the discussion. **Take notes.**

Step Seven:
Application:
Leader says, "Given all that we have learned, how will we each apply these lessons specifically and practically in our day to day family life?" Allow each person to respond.

THE FAMILY
REFORMATION PROJECT

FAMILY LEGACY EQ PROTOCOL

Family Legacy-
Love Without Hooks EQ Tool

The purpose of The Love Without Hooks EQ Tool™ is to equip the family with a process for experiencing the restoring power of forgiveness and unconditional love while setting themselves free from the torment of unforgiveness. There are few things that shut us off from each other faster and divide us more deeply than unforgiveness. To maintain an environment of safety, trust, support, forgiveness, love, purpose, and fun in the family, forgiveness and properly managing our expectations is mandatory.

Step One:

Select a leader (dad or mom) and then gather the family after a great meal in a relaxed environment. This exercise can be done in a face to face manner for best results, or over video app if need be. Have the leader read or share the purpose for the exercise written above.

Step Two:

Review:
Leader says, "Matthew 18:21-35 in the Bible contains the parable of the unmerciful servant. It is the story about a man who was forgiven a great debt and set free, only then to go and demand that someone who owed him a small debt be thrown into jail for not paying it. He was then thrown back into jail to be *tormented* because he would not release the debt of what someone owed him."

Leader says, "Bottom line: If we hold debts and keep demands of what other people "owe" us, God will deliver us to be tormented based on our choice to not forgive the debt.

CULTURAL ARCHITECTS

Step Three:

Instructions:
Leader says, "In a moment, I am going to pass out a sheet of paper to everyone along with a pen. On the paper is a series of questions that we are all going to write down our answers to individually. We will have 45 minutes to complete our answers to the questions. Please do not skip any questions. If you don't understand the question, please come to me and ask for help. If we near the end of our time and we are not complete, we may add an additional 15 minutes to complete our answers."
"I will play some soft instrumental music over a Bluetooth speaker while we are answering the questions. Finally, I'll lead everyone through an exercise, and we will process the exercise together in a debrief once we have completed the process."

Leader says, "Are there any questions before we start?" Leader answers questions
Leader hands out copies of the Love Without Hooks EQ Tool Questions (Next Page)

Step Four:

Love Without Hooks EQ Tool Questions
(Make copies and give to everyone with pen)

List the names of all those who I have unforgiveness towards, expectations on, or a demand that they "owe me" something.

```



```

Write the specific expectations I have on these people or what do I think they "owe me"?

```



```

If I have unforgiveness towards myself. What do I owe myself? What am I demanding?

```



```

What am I expecting of God or demanding that God owes me?

```



```

How do I feel when I do not get what I think I am owed from the lists above?

```



```

How do I feel when my expectations are not met?

How do I feel when I don't get these needs / wants met?

What do I do when I don't get what I am owed? How do I cope with lists above?

Describe the torment, pain, emotion, suffering that is present in the lists above.

How long will I choose to suffer over these things? How are these working for me?

What is keeping me from just letting all of this go? What keeps me from forgiving all?

Definition of Forgiveness- to pardon, to absolve, to give up all claim on account of

Step Five:

Exercise:
Leader says, "To release those who owe us rightfully or not, is to set them free and to set us free from torment. It is also scary because then we have nothing to guarantee the outcomes we've been counting on. It seems like giving up and losing the very things that we need or are owed. Therefore, we must surrender and trust that God, not people, is just and good and will take care of everything we truly need."

Instructions:
Leader says, "In a moment, we are all going to do some serious soul business and forgive all of those who we have unforgiveness towards. This is a personal thing and maybe even a private thing for many of us. When I give the word, I invite all of you to walk through the names on your list one by one, and to let go of the demand for whatever debt you feel they owe you. I'll show you how."

CULTURAL ARCHITECTS

Leader writes up on a flipchart the following just as it appears below.

"I choose to forgive and let go of _____(put in what you are letting go) that I have been holding onto when it comes to _____(name of the person) I forgive them of this debt right now for good and in so doing, I free myself from torment as well."

Leader says, "go through this statement, from the heart, for each and every person on your list including yourself and God."

Leader says, "For example, I choose to forgive and let go of (my demand for an apology) (put in what you are letting go) that I have been holding onto when it comes to (John Doe) (name of the person) I forgive them of this debt right now for good and in so doing, I free myself from torment as well.'

Step Six:
Debrief and Learning:
Leader bring everyone back together and say, "Let's talk about what we learned by everyone joining me is a discussion that addresses a few key questions one at a time."

1. What did you learn about unforgiveness?
2. What did you learn about forgiveness?
3. How did it feel to let it all go?

Allow ample amount of time for everyone to respond to the discussion. **Take notes.**

Step Seven:
Application:
Leader says, "Given all that we have learned, how will we each apply these lessons specifically and practically in our day to day family life?" Allow each person to respond.

CULTURAL ARCHITECTS

FAMILY LEGACY EQ PROTOCOL

Family Legacy-
The Powerful / Powerless EQ Tool

THE FAMILY
REFORMATION PROJECT

The purpose of the Powerful / Powerless EQ Tool™ is to equip the family with a process to live a powerful and impactful life from a place of personal responsibility. To choose to experience life through a *powerful* lens of dreams, growth, happiness and possibility instead of choosing to experience life through a *powerless* lens of excuses, blame, hopelessness and settling for less. Your family legacy is dramatically impacted by your choice between the powerful and powerless mindsets.

Step One:

Select a leader (dad or mom) and then gather the family after a great meal in a relaxed environment. This exercise can be done in a face to face manner for best results, or over video app if need be. Have the leader read or share the purpose for the exercise written above.

Step Two:

Review:
Leader says, "Have you ever been a victim? Have you ever found yourself in a set of circumstance that you didn't deserve to be in that are out of your control? Have you ever experienced undeserved betrayal, rejection, or abuse? Have you ever been the victim of theft, false accusation, a non-fault car accident or a violent crime? Most of us have vivid recollections of these kinds of victim experiences where we feel powerless.

Leader says, "Victim experiences tend to produce *powerless mindsets* that reinforce the belief that life happens to me not from me and that I am just along for the ride. These deeply implanted lenses cause individuals to see the world with the shades of:
- I'm not in control
- I'm not safe
- It's hopeless
- I can't recover
- I am powerless to change my circumstances"

Leaders says, "We can choose to see these experiences through a different lens, a *powerful* lens. If I choose to believe that life happens from me instead of to me, then I realize I can choose to look through a powerful lens at my life experiences and see my life through shades of:
- I'm am in control and personally responsible
- I'm as safe as I choose to be
        (Continued on next page)

(Continued on next page)

Step Two: (Continued)

- I can recover
- I am powerful to change my circumstances"

"Most important take away, **IT IS A CHOICE!**"

Step Three:

Instructions:
Caution: Use discretion. If there has been abuse or victimization of a family member by a family member, you may decide not to do this with both present or not at all on your own. Contact our office for help.

Leader says, "In a moment we are going to pair off in groups of two partners. I will lead us through some questions together and have you talk about some of them with your partner. I will also be writing certain responses up on the flipchart for us to look at together."

Leader says, "Go ahead and find your partner now and sit beside them where you can talk and hear each other."

Step Four:

Exercise:
Leader says, "Ok everyone, close your eyes for a moment, I want you to remember a time in your life when you felt *powerless* (like a victim). A time when someone did something that hurt you and you didn't deserve it. (Leader Pause for 10 seconds) I want you to specifically think about the feelings you had when this event happened to you. I'm going to give you 60 seconds of silence for you to get in touch with your feelings around when this happened." (leader wait 60 seconds)

Leader says, "Ok, you can open your eyes now. I am going to give you each 3 minutes to share your powerless victim story with your partner (especially how it felt)" "Partner one you will share first. Partner two you will not speak you are listening empathetically only. I will stop you when 3 minutes is up. Partner one, begin."

Leader give them 3 minutes and then say, "Thank you, Partner one you can stop talking. Partner two it is now your turn to share your powerless victim story especially how it felt. Partner one you are now the listener, Partner two 3 minutes, begin."

Leader give them 3 minutes and then say, "Thank you, Partner two you can stop talking."

Leader- now move to the flipchart paper where you will draw the illustration exactly as it appears below.

Leader says, "Tell me how it felt as you told your story? How did you feel?"

Leader: List the feelings that members share in the powerless section below.

Powerless | Powerful
               |
               |
               |
               |
               |
               |

Exercise:

Leader says, "Thank you for being vulnerable and authentic in sharing your feelings from a difficult time in your lives. Look at the feelings we have written down up here… The darker feelings we experience in these times can often attach themselves to some powerless mindsets and for good reason. But they don't have to. We have a choice of what we decide to think, believe and agree with. Let me show you what I mean."

Leader, Pull out a spiral bound school notebook that has a brown cardboard colored back cover and a bright colored front cover. You can find one at any store that has school supplies.

Hold the notebook between one set of partners so that they are each seeing a different side of the notebook, one is seeing the front cover and the other is seeing the back cover.

Leader says, "This notebook represents the powerless story you just shared, partner one, what color is this notebook? (let them respond and repeat response) "blue" yes, Partner two, what color is this notebook? (let them respond and repeat response) "brown" yes. Wait a minute, the story you just told represented by this notebook is blue or is it brown? The answer is, **"it depends on which perspective you look at it"**

Leader says, "In a moment you are each going to share the same story but from a different perspective. Instead of brown, this time it will be told from a blue perspective. Instead of telling about that event from a powerless viewpoint, you are going to share it from a powerful viewpoint.

Leader says, "Partner one, you are first. Now share the same story from a *powerful* perspective using, "I chose…" over and over. I chose to …..

CULTURAL ARCHITECTS

Make a list of feelings in the Powerful section below:

Powerless | Powerful
          |
          |
          |
          |
          |
          |

What are the costs and benefits of the Powerless perspective?
Costs:

What are the costs and benefits of the Powerful perspective?
Costs:

Benefits:

Choice moving forward?

THE FAMILY
REFORMATION PROJECT

FAMILY LEGACY EMOTIONAL INTELLIGENCE PROTOCOL

Family Legacy- Personality Profile Tool (Free Tool)

NOTE: There are additional tools and reports available for a small fee through our office from The Everything DiSC™ by Wiley* suite of analytics. See the end of this free tool for more information about these leading personality EQ analytical tools for your family.

The purpose of this tool is to provide the family with a free basic process for understanding each family members unique personality type and the implications that come along with it. This tool will help family members explore their own unique design along with others in the family unit. With this expanded knowledge and increased empathy, family members will engage in conversations to better understand, relate, communicate, and empathize with family members.

Step One:

Select a leader (dad or mom) and then gather the family after a great meal in a relaxed environment. This exercise can be done in a face to face manner for best results, or over video app if need be. Have the leader read or share the purpose for the exercise written above.

Step Two:

Review

Leader says, "Your personality is a part of the answer to the question, "Who am I." This Family Personality Profile tool will help us understand personality preferences such as whether you are more:
- Task driven or relationship driven
- Fast or slow paced
- Extroverted or introverted energy
- Methodical or spontaneous
- Precise or innovative
- Challenging or accepting
- Decisive or analytical
- Expressive or contemplative

Leader says, "Our analysis will show us where our predispositions and assumptions are, our blind spots, along with those of other family members. The benefit is that we can then choose to know and respect the design of every individual and use this information to improve our family relationships."

CULTURAL ARCHITECTS

Step Three:

Explore the DISC Diagram
Leader reads through entire diagram and helps members identify where they fit on it.

The graphic below provides a snapshot of the four basic DiSC® styles.

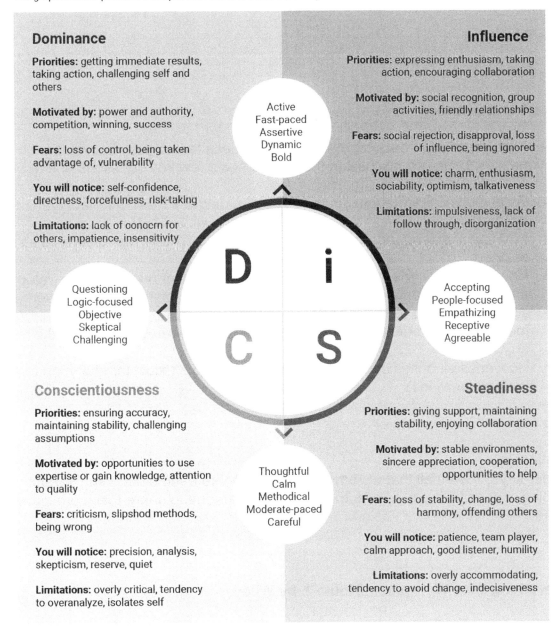

Dominance

Priorities: getting immediate results, taking action, challenging self and others

Motivated by: power and authority, competition, winning, success

Fears: loss of control, being taken advantage of, vulnerability

You will notice: self-confidence, directness, forcefulness, risk-taking

Limitations: lack of concern for others, impatience, insensitivity

Influence

Priorities: expressing enthusiasm, taking action, encouraging collaboration

Motivated by: social recognition, group activities, friendly relationships

Fears: social rejection, disapproval, loss of influence, being ignored

You will notice: charm, enthusiasm, sociability, optimism, talkativeness

Limitations: impulsiveness, lack of follow through, disorganization

Active
Fast-paced
Assertive
Dynamic
Bold

Questioning
Logic-focused
Objective
Skeptical
Challenging

Accepting
People-focused
Empathizing
Receptive
Agreeable

Conscientiousness

Priorities: ensuring accuracy, maintaining stability, challenging assumptions

Motivated by: opportunities to use expertise or gain knowledge, attention to quality

Fears: criticism, slipshod methods, being wrong

You will notice: precision, analysis, skepticism, reserve, quiet

Limitations: overly critical, tendency to overanalyze, isolates self

Thoughtful
Calm
Methodical
Moderate-paced
Careful

Steadiness

Priorities: giving support, maintaining stability, enjoying collaboration

Motivated by: stable environments, sincere appreciation, cooperation, opportunities to help

Fears: loss of stability, change, loss of harmony, offending others

You will notice: patience, team player, calm approach, good listener, humility

Limitations: overly accommodating, tendency to avoid change, indecisiveness

Leader makes copies of the diagram and gives one to everyone as a handout and says, "Let's read one section at a time and identify which family members fit in each one. D – I – S – C"

Step Three: continued

Leader says, "As we cover each section, draw a dot for each person in the section you think best describes them. One dot per person in the section that best describes them. Include one for yourself. Write the initials of the person beside their dot."

Have Fun!

Step Four:

Debrief and Learning

Leader bring everyone back together and say, "Let's talk about what we learned by everyone joining me is a discussion that addresses a few key questions one at a time."

1. What did you learn about yourself from the diagram? (allow for everyone to answer)
2. What did you learn about others from the diagram? (allow everyone to share their answers)
3. How does what you learned connect to the character qualities, core values, and purpose in our family identity? (allow for everyone to share their answers)
4. What can you do to better connect, communicate, and understand other family members based on what you learned? (allow for everyone to share their answers)
5. How does all of this connect to our family Legacy? (allow for everyone to share their connections)

Step Five:

Application:
Leader says, "Given all that we have learned, how are each of us going to apply the learning in specific ways in the future?" (allow everyone to share their commitments to action

End

*Everything Disc Workplace Profile™ by Wiley

The Everything DiSC Workplace Profile and Comparison Reports from Wiley Publishers are one of many EQ tools available through our office. They are inexpensive and extremely helpful. Contact our office if you would like more information.

Create more effective and productive family relationships
Uses: Team building, communication, conflict management, motivation, productivity, personal development, empathy.

CULTURAL /\RCHITECTS

*Everything Disc Workplace Profile™ by Wiley (continued)

It's not just about me; it's about our relationships.
- Gain insights into your own behavior and that of others.
- Understand and appreciate the styles of the people you work with.
- Learn how to make communication more effective.
- Create strategies for overcoming challenges when working with people of different DiSC® styles.

Features of the Workplace Profile (transferable to a family context)
- Profile is for one person.
- Appropriate for ANYONE 12 and over
- 20-page workplace-specific report that focuses on your priorities and strengths as well as those of others. (transferable to a family context)
- Provides clear strategies for building more effective relationships.
- The language of the narrative is supportive, personalized and easily understood without the intervention of an assessment professional.
- Takes 15-20 minutes to complete the survey. Assessment results are available upon completion.

This tool will create one-on-one personality comparisons between pairings of all family members with insights and recommendations for improving each relationship.

$60*   Per person and includes both individual profile and Comparison Reports
$275* Per person - Profile + 2 -1-hour group coaching calls
        (unlimited number of people)
$425* Profile + 2 -1-hour personal Coaching calls (one person)

Contact our office if you would like more information

FAMILY LEGACY IDENTITY PROTOCOL

Family Legacy-
Identity Protocol 2

THE FAMILY
REFORMATION PROJECT

The Purpose of The Family Legacy Identity Protocol™ is to discover together your family identity and uniqueness: past, present, and future while growing in the understanding of each individual's unique personality. Together, you will establish the family character, core values, and purpose, which determine legacy, and create a family coat of arms. Engaging everyone in this process will equip the next generation to do the same.

I've said that the only legacy I leave is the one I live, and I believe it's true. However, It may be an even deeper truth to say that the only legacy I live is the one that, *"I am"*. This is an important distinction. If the ultimate legacy is the character and nature of our Designer (Who He is) passed on to His Son and then built inside of every other child of His over a lifetime, then my legacy is *who I am* expressed through the life I live.

In the end, it takes what it takes! I suggest it takes **four key experiences** for any individual to discover and "know" their true identity. This is true for myself and the thousands of people I've worked with over three decades. When a family has these experiences together, the family "knows" their true identity as well. The framework for the Identity protocols is designed with these experiences in mind.

1. *An authentic search*
2. *A revelation*
3. *A choice to believe*
4. *An unwavering commitment to inside out action*

The Family Legacy Identity Protocol™ is a set of exercises that equip the family with a process to discover together the family identity and uniqueness: past, present, and future while growing in the understanding of each individual's unique personality. Together, you will establish the family character, core values, and purpose, which determine legacy, and create a family coat of arms. Once the family identity is clear, intentionally living the legacy and passing it on to the generations becomes possible.

The experiential exercises for the **Family Legacy Identity Protocol**™ below are insightful, unifying and empowering. They are designed to create deep connection between family members past, present and future by identifying the *family identity, character, core values, and purpose* which **are the real legacy** of the family line.

CULTURAL ARCHITECTS

The Family Legacy Identity Protocol™ *framework* flows out of the *four key experiences* required to "know" your true identity that I mentioned in the last section.

An authentic search with an open heart and mind where I examine "who I am" in light of:
- True identity from the Creator as designed (the design)
- Family history (the context for my existence)
- Genetic history (the facts and science)
- Generational history (the flows)
- Inner healing (healing identity wounds)
- DISC Profiles, personality types, and styles (the analytics)
- Family characteristics, core values, and purpose (the why)
- Affirmations and the creation of a Family Coat of Arms

A revelation
- An eye opener to see and know something never seen or known before (an AHA!)
- An uncovering of understanding of true identity that's been hidden

A choice to believe (to agree, faith)
- In my identity (as I think in my heart so am I)
- In my purpose
- In the purpose of my family line past, present and future
- In my personal responsibility to steward my life and legacy

An unwavering commitment to inside out action with a coach approach
- The coach approach to stewarding your identity and your legacy

CULTURAL ARCHITECTS

THE FAMILY
REFORMATION PROJECT

FAMILY LEGACY IDENTITY PROTOCOL

Family Legacy-
True Identity Tool

The purpose of this tool is to provide a process for seeing where the current understanding of family members is when it comes to a sense of their own identity. A simple set of questions below will probe each family members thinking around their identity.

This exercise will open up an awareness of the characteristics, values, talents, and purpose for family members and for the family as a whole. You may need to modify as needed for young children but, include them. The formation of identity and a growing sense of positive self-awareness is important for us no matter our age.

Step One:

Select a leader (dad or mom) and then gather the family after a great meal in a relaxed environment. This exercise can be done in a face to face manner for best results, or over video app if need be. Have the leader read or share the purpose for the exercise written above.

Step Two:

Instructions:
Leader says, **"In a moment, we are going to each answer a set of questions individually on paper** as we address our current understanding of our "true identity" and answer the question, "Who am I?" I will give you the questions, one at a time, and I want each of you to write down your responses as they come to you. We will process our answers together in a debrief once we have completed the process."

Step Three:

Questions:
Leader says, "Question number one, question, Who are you? Write down whatever comes to mind. Take all the time you need. Begin." _____

Leader: take the appropriate amount of time to allow members to mindfully complete their answers to the question.

Leader says, "Question number two, question, What does your Designer say about who you are? Write down your responses on the paper." _____

CULTURAL ARCHITECTS

Step Three: (continued)

Questions:
Leader: take the appropriate amount of time to allow members to mindfully complete their answers to the question. (special consideration may be required for younger children)

Leader says, "Question number three, question, "What character qualities would you say describe you best?" _____

Leader: take the appropriate amount of time to allow members to mindfully complete their answers to the question.

Questions:
Leader says, "Question number four, question, What are your natural skills, learned skills and spiritual skills or competencies? Write down what you are good at in these three areas. Take all the time you need. Begin." _____

Leader: take the appropriate amount of time to allow members to mindfully complete their answers to the question.

Leader says, "Question number five, question, What are you passionate about? Write down your responses on the paper." _____

Leader: take the appropriate amount of time to allow members to mindfully complete their answers to the question.

Leader says, "Question number six, question, What is your current understanding of your purpose or design? Write My purpose is _____ "

Leader: take the appropriate amount of time to allow members to mindfully complete their answers to the question

Step Four:

Debrief and Learning:
Leader bring everyone back together and say, "Let's talk about what we learned by everyone joining me is a discussion that addresses a few key questions one at a time."

1. What did you learn as you answered the questions? (allow for everyone to share their answers)
2. What is you level of confidence and clarity around your true identity on a scale of 1 (low) and 10 (high) and why? (allow for everyone to share their answers)
3. What are you learning about each other as you share your answers? (allow for everyone to share their answers)

Step Four: (continued)

Debrief and Learning:

4. What are everyone's thoughts about the answer to this question, what is the purpose of our family? (allow for everyone to make their commitments to the family)

Remember: This exercise is to gain a preliminary and current understanding of individual and family identity and purpose.

Step Five:

Application:
Leader says, "Given all that we have learned, how will we each apply these lessons specifically in our lives day to day moving forward?" Allow each person to respond.

CULTURAL /\RCHITECTS

THE FAMILY
REFORMATION PROJECT

FAMILY LEGACY IDENTITY PROTOCOL

Family Legacy-
Family History Tool

The purpose of this tool is to provide your family with a process for connecting you to each other and giving you a context for identity by exploring the general history of your family. Through researching your family history, gathering the stories of generations past, and sharing your thoughtful observations of your findings, you will have a new dimension of understanding around family identity. You will also pass on your discoveries to your children for posterity.

This tool is the first of three exercises that guide you through the exploration of the family history and include the sharing of what you discover. You choose how deep and detailed of a search you want to do. Parents, most of this work falls to you.

Instructions:

This tool and process is different from most of the other tools in that it may require more time, people, and effort to complete. If you are fortunate enough to have ancestors who took it upon themselves to gather, document, and pass down any family history, this is the perfect time to pull it out, dust it off and examine it. If not, go to work online, interviewing older family members still alive, or use one of the online services available to assist you like Ancestry.com.

This tool has a five-step process for connecting your family history to your family identity and your family legacy.

1. Exploration and Research
2. Distilling the Legacy
3. Reporting the findings
4. Debrief and Learning
5. Application- governing the good bad and ugly

Step One:

Exploration and Research

If you are taking the lead on this as the leader, I recommend that you enlist the help of other family members. It is important to set some parameters around your search or you could literally take a lifetime in exploring the details of multiple generations and not complete the goal of this exercise, connecting your family history to your family identity and your family legacy.

CULTURAL ARCHITECTS

Step One: (continued)

Research Recommendations:
First, determine what you are looking for so that you recognize it when you find it.
To avoid wasting time and wild goose chases, review materials, hold conversations, and listen to stories looking for the following in your family history:

Exploration and Research

- Skills, trades, and patterns of behavior in business, faith, enterprises
- Gifts and talents that came naturally
- Passions and interests
- Roles and careers
- Character qualities
- Challenges and failures
- Achievements and honors
- Sense of humor and funny stories
- Stories of value (risk, character, values)

Second, once you set your sites on what you are looking for, locate the research that anyone in your family line has already done and review it. **Take good notes or video if possible.**

Third, conduct interviews of the oldest family members with special attention given to asking them questions from the bullet list above. Take good notes or video if possible.

Fourth, based on what the above actions yield, conduct some good ole research online.

Fifth, you may consider using an online family research tool to aide you in your exploration. Remember to keep an eye on what you are looking for as listed above.

Hidden is plain sight and on display in the telling of the family stories are the clues to identity, purpose and legacy.

Step Two:

Distilling the Legacy
What I mean here is to take the mountain of research and go through it a few times to pull out the character qualities, core values, and purpose of your family history from the mass detail.

From all the research, what have you identified as the short list of your historical
Legacy Narrative:
- Family Character Qualities
- Family Core Values
- Family Purpose

CULTURAL ⋀RCHITECTS

Step two: (continued)

Distilling the Legacy

Once you have the lists, select a handful of the most interesting stories that illustrate the family character qualities, core values and purpose and prepare to share them with the family in a two-hour sitting. You may go longer, of course, but make sure you draw out the relevant items to connect family history to family identity and family Legacy. Enjoy!
The Family History Tool

Step Three:

Reporting the Findings

Now that you have completed all of the research and distilled it down to the most important legacy items, it's time to gather everyone together and share your findings. Remember, this is an intentional sharing that focuses on the *Legacy Narrative* out of all the narratives you could convey.

You may decide to complete all three Family History Tools before gathering everyone together for reporting the findings. Then you could share all three back-to-back for a special day experience of the Family General History, Family Genetic History, and the Family Generational History.

Leader, gather everyone together along with all of your findings and the stories you've prepared to tell. Then share! You may invite others who have helped with the research to help out with the storytelling.

In your sharing, be sure that you frame your shares in the context of the Legacy Narrative and in this case, the general family history details.

Organize your reporting and shares around your Family History **Legacy Narrative:**
- Family Character Qualities
- Family Core Values
- Family Purpose

Sharing the specifics of the research and stories below in the framework of the **Legacy Narrative:**

- Skills, trades, and patterns of behavior in business, faith, enterprises
- Gifts and talents that came naturally
- Passions and interests
- Roles and careers
- Character qualities
- Challenges and failures

CULTURAL ARCHITECTS

Step Three: (continued)

Legacy Narrative:

- Achievements and honors
- Sense of humor and funny stories
- Stories of value (risk, character, values)

If you've prepared your Legacy Narrative well, it should be no problem for the family to recount the narrative back to you in the Learning and Debrief Step.

Step Four:

Debrief and Learning:
Leader bring everyone back together and say, "Let's talk about what we learned by everyone joining me is a discussion that addresses a few key questions one at a time."

1. What did you learn about the character qualities in our family history? (allow for everyone to share their answers)
2. What did you learn about the core values in our family history? (allow for everyone to share their answers)
3. What did you learn about the purpose of our family or family line from our family history? (allow for everyone to share their answers)
4. How are these all connected to our family identity? To who we are as a family? (allow for everyone to share their connections)
5. How are these all connected to our family Legacy? (allow for everyone to share their connections)

Step Five:

Application:
Leader says, "Given all that we have learned, how will we each apply the learning in our day to day family life?" Allow each person to respond.

This is a profound exercise and multi-generational impact. Passing on the history in the framework of a Legacy Narrative and teaching our children to do the same is a game changer!

CULTURAL /\RCHITECTS

THE FAMILY
REFORMATION PROJECT

FAMILY LEGACY IDENTITY PROTOCOL

Family Legacy-
Genetic History Tool

The purpose of this tool is to provide your family with a process for connecting you to each other and giving you a context for identity by exploring the genetic history of your family. Through researching your genetic history, gathering the facts and details of generations past, and sharing your thoughtful observations of your findings, you will have a new dimension of understanding around family identity. You will also pass on your discoveries to your children for posterity.

This is the second exercise in the Family History section of the Identity Protocol. You choose how deep and detailed of a search you want to do. Parents, most of this work falls to you.

Instructions:

This tool and process is different from most of the other tools in that it may require more time, people, and effort to complete. If you are fortunate enough to have ancestors who took it upon themselves to gather, document, and pass down any genetic family history, this is the perfect time to pull it out, dust it off and examine it. If not, go to work online, interviewing older family members still alive, or use one of the online services available to assist you like 23andme.com.

This tool has a five-step process for connecting your genetic family history to your family identity and your family legacy.

1. Exploration and Research
2. Distilling the Legacy
3. Reporting the findings
4. Debrief and Learning
5. Application- governing the good bad and ugly

Step One:

Exploration and Research

If you are taking the lead on this as the leader, I recommend that you enlist the help of other family members. It is important to set some parameters around your search or you could literally take a lifetime in exploring the details of multiple generations and not complete the goal of this exercise, connecting your genetic family history to your family identity and your family legacy.

CULTURAL ARCHITECTS

Step One: (continued)

Research Recommendations:
First, determine what you are looking for so that you recognize it when you find it.
To avoid wasting time and wild goose chases, review materials, hold conversations, and listen to stories looking for the following in your family genetic history:

- Geographic roots and tradition
- Medical history
- Available Genealogy
- Predispositions to addiction
- Physical features
- Adoptions
- Blended family details
- Facts unique to your family
- Allergies and food sensitivities
- Super powers

While these may appear to be "dry facts," they are important for the good stewardship of the family from generation to generation.

Second, once you set your sites on what you are looking for, locate the research that anyone in your family line has already done and review it. **Take good notes or video if possible.**

Third, conduct interviews of the oldest family members with special attention given to asking them questions from the bullet list above. Take good notes or video if possible.

Fourth, based on what the above actions yield, conduct some good ole research online.

Fifth, you may consider using an online genetic family research tool to aide you in your exploration. Remember to keep an eye on what you are looking for as listed above.

Step Two:

Distilling the Legacy
What I mean here is to take the mountain of research and go through it a few times to pull out the character qualities, core values, and purpose of your family genetic history from the mass detail.

From all the research, what have you identified as the short list of your genetic historical **Legacy Narrative:**
- Family Character Qualities
- Family Core Values
- Family Purpose

CULTURAL ARCHITECTS

Step Two: (continued)

Distilling the Legacy
In addition, you may make other valuable discoveries addressing how you may best steward your genetic family history well moving forward in key areas such as:

- Medical history
- Predispositions to addictions
- Allergies and food sensitivities

Once you have the lists, select a handful of the most relevant facts, discoveries, and stories. Then, prepare to share them with the family in a two-hour sitting. You may go longer, of course, but make sure you draw out the relevant items to connect family history to family identity and family Legacy. It is also important communicate the raw detail of the genetic legacy that is relevant for generations to come.

Step Three:
Reporting the Findings

Now that you have completed all of the research and distilled it down to the most important legacy items, it's time to gather everyone together and share your findings. Remember, this is an intentional sharing that focuses on the **Legacy Narrative** along with the most relevant genetic family history.

You may decide to complete all three Family History Tools before gathering everyone together for reporting the findings. Then you could share all three back-to-back for a special day experience of the Family General History, Family Genetic History, and the Family Generational History.

Leader, gather everyone together along with all of your findings, facts, and stories you've prepared to tell. Then share! You may invite others who have helped with the research to help out with the storytelling.

In your sharing, be sure that you frame your shares in the context of the Legacy Narrative and in this case, the genetic family history details.

Organize your reporting and shares around your Family History **Legacy Narrative**:

- Family Character Qualities
- Family Core Values
- Family Purpose

Sharing the specifics of the research and stories below in the framework of the **Legacy Narrative:**

- Predispositions to addiction
- Physical features
- Adoptions

Step Three: (continued)

Legacy Narrative:
- Blended family details
- Facts unique to your family
- Allergies and food sensitivities
- Super powers

If you've prepared your Legacy Narrative well, it should be no problem for the family to recount the narrative back to you in the Learning and Debrief Step.

Family Genetic History Tool

Step Four:

Debrief and Learning:
Leader bring everyone back together and say, "Let's talk about what we learned by everyone joining me in a discussion that addresses a few key questions one at a time."

1. What did you learn about the character qualities in our genetic family history? (allow for everyone to share their answers)
2. What did you learn about the core values in our genetic family history? (allow for everyone to share their answers)
3. What did you learn about relevant genetic factors to steward from our genetic family history? (allow for everyone to share their answers)
4. How are these all connected to our family identity? To who we are as a family? (allow for everyone to share their connections)
5. How are these all connected to our family Legacy? (allow for everyone to share their connections)

Step Five:

Application:
Leader says, "Given all that we have learned, how will we each apply the learning in our day to day family life?" Allow each person to respond.

This is a profound exercise and multi-generational impact. Passing on the genetic history in the framework of a Legacy Narrative and teaching our children to do the same is a game changer!

CULTURAL /\RCHITECTS

FAMILY LEGACY IDENTITY PROTOCOL

Family Legacy- Generational History Tool

THE FAMILY
REFORMATION PROJECT

The purpose of this tool is to provide your family with a process for connecting you to each other and giving you a context for family identity by conveying the intellectual, emotional, and especially, spiritual flows that have influenced your family from generations prior up to today. Many of the problems that we are working to resolve in our own lives today are actually rooted in generational choices and patterns of behavior from family past. These generational "flows" influence us through our genetic link to the past.

This tool is the third of three exercises that guide you through the exploration of the family history and include the sharing of what you discover. You choose how deep and detailed of a search you want to do. Parents, most of this work falls to you.

Instructions:

This tool and process is different from most of the other tools in that it may require more time, people, and effort to complete. If you are fortunate enough to have ancestors who took it upon themselves to gather, document, and pass down any family history, this is the perfect time to pull it out, dust it off and examine it. If not, go to work online, interviewing older family members still alive, or even praying and listening for revelation.

This tool has a five-step process for connecting your family generational history to your family identity and your family legacy. It will also reveal opportunities for healing and growth.

1. Exploration and Research
2. Distilling the Legacy
3. Reporting the findings
4. Debrief and Learning
5. Application- governing the good bad and ugly

Step One:

Exploration and Research

If you are taking the lead on this as the leader, I recommend that you enlist the help of other family members. It is important to set some parameters around your search or you could literally take a lifetime in exploring the details of multiple generations and not complete the goal of this exercise, connecting your family generational history to your family identity and your family legacy. This exercise adds the opportunity for healing and growth.

Step One: (continued)

Research Recommendations:
First, determine what you are looking for so that you recognize it when you find it.
To avoid wasting time and wild goose chases, review materials, hold conversations, and listen to stories looking for the following in your family generational history: **Family Generational History Tool**

The truth is, we are ultimately personally responsible for the choices we make that drive the results in each of our lives. And, it is also true that there are flows of both good and bad generational influences that do affect our daily lives to varying degrees. Identifying these influences is the first step to stopping the unhealthy flows and embracing the healthy flows as we resolve and steward these influences while we are on our watch for a better tomorrow for our generations downstream. We have a responsibility to clean up the litter in the generational stream before it continues to our children.

These influences may be good or bad and may include flows of:

- Lust
- Early death
- Addiction
- Criminal behavior
- Vulnerability to deceptions
- Violence
- Justice
- Leadership
- Wealth
- Poverty
- Mental illness
- Barrenness
- Innovation
- Creativity
- Faith
- Fear
- Sexual perversion
- Secret society involvement
- Philanthropy
- Other intellectual, emotional, and spiritual flows, patterns of thinking, behavior, etc.

Second, once you set your sights on what you are looking for, locate the research that anyone in your family line has already done and review it. Take good notes or video if possible.

Third, conduct interviews of the oldest family members with special attention given to asking them questions from the bullet list above. Take good notes or video if possible.

CULTURAL /\RCHITECTS

Step One: (continued)

Exploration and Research

Fourth, based on what the above actions yield, conduct some good ole research online.

Fifth, Go to the Lord in prayer and ask for eyes to see the "flows" at work in you and your family line. Remember to keep an eye on what you are looking for as listed above.

Hidden in plain sight and on display in the telling of the family stories are the clues to identity, purpose and legacy.

Step Two:

Distilling the Legacy
What I mean here is to take the mountain of research and go through it a few times to pull out the character qualities, core values, and purpose of your family history from the mass detail. In this exercise, you will also pull out the "flows" that you notice.

From all the research, what have you identified as the short list of your generational historical **Legacy Narrative:**
- Family Character Qualities
- Family Core Values
- Family Purpose
- The good and bad generational "flows" that you uncovered

Once you have the lists, select a handful of the most interesting stories that illustrate the family character qualities, core values, purpose, and generational flows (good, bad , and ugly) and prepare to share them with the family in a two-hour sitting. You may go longer, of course, but make sure you draw out the relevant items to connect family history to family identity and family Legacy. This exercise has special attention given to the generational flows.

Step Three:

Reporting the Findings

Now that you have completed all of the research and distilled it down to the most important legacy items, it's time to gather everyone together and share your findings. Remember, this is an intentional sharing that focuses on the **Legacy Narrative** out of all the narratives you could convey.

You may decide to complete all three Family History Tools before gathering everyone together for reporting the findings. Then you could share all three back-to-back for a special day experience of the Family General History, Family Genetic History, and the Family Generational History.

CULTURAL ⋀RCHITECTS

Step Three: (continued)

Reporting the Findings

Leader, gather everyone together along with all of your findings and the stories you've prepared to tell. Then share! You may invite others who have helped with the research to help out with the storytelling.

In your sharing, be sure that you frame your shares in the context of the Legacy Narrative and in this case, the generational family history details.

Organize your reporting and shares around your Family History **Legacy Narrative:**
- Family Character Qualities
- Family Core Values
- Family Purpose
- The good and bad generational "flows" that you uncovered

Sharing the specifics of the research and stories below in the framework of the **Legacy Narrative:** The generational influences may be good or bad and may include flows of:

- Lust
- Early death
- Addiction
- Criminal behavior
- Vulnerability to deceptions
- Violence
- Justice
- Leadership
- Wealth
- Poverty
- Mental illness
- Barrenness
- Innovation
- Creativity
- Faith
- Fear
- Sexual perversion
- Secret society involvement
- Philanthropy
- Other intellectual, emotional, and spiritual flows, patterns of thinking, behavior, etc.

If you've prepared your Legacy Narrative well, it should be no problem for the family to recount the narrative back to you in the Learning and Debrief Step.

CULTURAL ARCHITECTS

Step Four:

Debrief and Learning:
Leader bring everyone back together and say, "Let's talk about what we learned by everyone joining me in a discussion that addresses a few key questions one at a time."

1. What did you learn about the character qualities, core values, and purpose in our family generational history? (allow for everyone to share their answers)
2. What did you learn about the good and healthy generational flows in your family line? (allow for everyone to share their answers)
3. What did you learn about the bad and unhealthy generational flows in your family line? (allow for everyone to share their answers)
4. How are the flows connected to our family identity? To who we are as a family? (allow for everyone to share their connections)
5. How are these all connected to our family Legacy? (allow for everyone to share their connections)

Step Five:

Application:
Leader says, "Given all that we have learned, we are each going to apply the learning in a specific way now and in the future."

Leader says, "Stewarding our agreement and disagreement with the generational flows is how we open up the flows of the good and healthy and shut off the flows of the bad and unhealthy." We do this with our own words and voice by making a declaration out loud that engages our mind, will, emotion, and spirit to govern (direct the flows) in our family line.

Leader says, "We want to open up the flows of the good we uncovered in our generational family history exercise." By declaring with our own words and our own voice that,

"I agree with and open up the generational flow of _____. (name specifically the good flow here e.g. kindness, philanthropy, love, leadership, etc.) in me and my family line."

(Go through each of the healthy flows one at a time and open them up)

Leader says, "We want to shut off the flows of the bad we uncovered in our generational family history exercise." By declaring with our own words and our own voice that,

"I disagree with and shut off the generational flow of _____ (name specifically the bad flow here e.g. lust, poverty, violence, addiction, divorce, etc.) in me and my family line."

(Go through each of the unhealthy flows one at a time and shut them off)

Step Five: (continued)

Application:

NOTE:

This exercise, by design, is addressing deeply engrained patterns of thinking, behaviors, and spiritual flows that have influenced your family line for generations. We have the opportunity to heal, resolve, and reconcile the unhealthy flows in a way that will alter the course of the generations who follow us. While this tool provides a simple and powerful start to this process, there is more work to be done here.

I want to encourage you to do two things:

1. Use the inner healing exercise and tool as a next step in addressing the unhealthy generational flows.
2. Reach out to our office if you find difficulty in facilitating these processes and in achieving a breakthrough.

This is a profound exercise with a multi-generational impact. Governing and stewarding the generational flows and teaching our children to do the same is a legacy changer!

FAMILY LEGACY IDENTITY PROTOCOL

Family Legacy-
Inner Healing Tool

THE FAMILY
REFORMATION PROJECT

The purpose of this tool is to provide the family with a process for the inner healing of identity soul wounds that are undermining the abundant life and legacy that you were designed for. When these wounds are healed, we literally remove our vulnerability to being manipulated by them. Once healed, we no longer experience the unhealthy flow of influence into our mind, will, emotions, and spirit effectively stopping the flow. This directly impacts our generations downstream.

Review:
There are multiple inner healing models delivered through a variety of healing modalities. Far too many to dive into here. However, most all of the models have a very basic framework for healing that nearly anyone can implement.

This simple inner healing framework is a process for discovering wounds, lies, and truth in an environment of love that leads to a choice to disagree with the lies (old way of thinking) and to agree with the truth.(new way of thinking) Once we choose (will) to change our thinking (mind), our feelings (emotions) amplify the new choice and thinking and a soul wound is healed.

This Inner Healing Tool will guide you through this *four-part inner healing model.*
- Reveal - identifying the lie, deception, and false accusation from the wound
- Repent - choosing to disagree with the lie and agree with the truth from the heart
- Renew - receiving grace, setting your mind, will, emotions, and spirit on a new path
- Restate - speaking out loud your new choices of thinking, believing and action

Please reach out to us if you recognize the need for support in healing these deep wounds.

Instructions:

It is important for the Leader to understand that while this inner healing model can be shared and taught to everyone as a group, it is more effectively executed by the Leader and one other person at a time. This allows for a measure of privacy and individual attention while allowing the Leader to focus on the process and the person focus on themselves.

CULTURAL ARCHITECTS

Step One:

Reveal: identifying the lie, deception, or false accusation from the wound

Part One

There are three places to start when asking the question, "Where do I need inner healing?" First, just notice and become aware of the pain, the dysfunctional behavior, the unhealthy emotions and the inapproriate reactions. Once you identify one, take that discovery into the rest of the healing process one at a time. (e.g. lust, unforgiveness, addiction, violence, fits of anger, fear, insecurity, isolation, anxiety, etc.)

Inner Healing Tool

The second place to start is to look at the list below and circle the unhealthy generational flows that you struggle with:

- Lust
- Early death
- Addiction
- Criminal behavior
- Vulnerability to deceptions
- Violence
- Poverty
- Mental illness
- Barrenness
- Fear
- Sexual perversion
- Secret society involvement
- Occultism
- Chronic physical pain
- Anxiety
- Depression
- Disease
- Rejection
- Suicidal thoughts
- Other intellectual, emotional, and spiritual flows, patterns of thinking, behavior, etc.

Once you've identified the unhealthy flows that you deal with, take those discoveries one at a time through the rest of the inner-healing process.

The third place to start is to pray and ask the lord for guidance in this process. Ask Him what issue He wants you to start with. Once you have a clear idea where He is leading, take that discovery into the rest of the inner-healing process one at a time.

Step One: (continued)

Part Two
Once you have identified an unhealthy flow such as, depression, go to the Lord with the following questions and wait on Him, listening for His answer. **Take notes.**

Questions for greater revelation:
- Father, when did this flow (depression) begin in my life or generations?
- Father, what do you want me to know about this flow of (depression) in my life?
- Father, what is the lie underneath this flow (depression) in my life?

Step Two:

Repent: choosing to disagree with the lie and agree with the truth from the heart

Once you have revelation around what wound and the resulting flow of unhealthy influence, its origins, the lies underneath of it, and what God wants you to know about it- You know your next steps toward healing which may include:

- Choosing to disagree with the lie and agree with the truth of God from the heart
- Choose to forgive the person who wounded you, may include your generations past.
- Choose to ask forgiveness for responding sinfully to the wound (bitterness, revenge, hate, etc.)
- Choose to forgive yourself for your part in wounding yourself in any way
- Choose to forgive God if you have blamed Him for the wounding in any way
- Choose to confess the sin and ask to be delivered from the unhealthy flow

It is critically important that you do not merely go through the motions and follow this tool without the corresponding authentic heart level buy in. The actions above must come from the heart to be effective and bring healing to your soul.

Take the time to go through this process for each and every unhealthy flow as needed. Reach out for help in you need it.

Step Three:

Renew: receiving grace, setting your mind, will, emotions, and spirit on a new path

Once you have disagreed with the lies from the heart, it's time to complete the change in your thinking. In order to be transformed, we must disagree with one way of thinking (lie) and agree with another way of thinking (Truth). This is called "renewing our mind" and is a vital part of transformation.

CULTURAL ARCHITECTS

Step Three: (continued)

Renew: receiving grace, setting your mind, will, emotions, and spirit on a new path

- Choose to receive grace and set your mind, will, emotions, and spirit on the Truth that directly overcomes the lie you formerly agreed with.
- Choose to agree with God's Word, the Truth and create a healthy flow of truth where there used to be an unhealthy flow of lies.
- Choose to speak and memorize a scripture or Truth that disempowers the former lies.
- Choose to ask the Holy Spirit to "lead you into all Truth" and He will help you.
- Choose to govern your mind by keeping agreement with the Truth

Again, this only works when you do it from your heart with authenticity and faith.
Inner Healing Tool

Step Four:
Restate: speaking out loud your new choices of thinking, believing and action

There is power in our words because they overflow from our hearts. It is one of the ways that we are most like God. We create with our words. The power of life and death are in the tongue. Our declarations of both good and bad, blessing and cursing have lasting and tangible impact on the seen and unseen world around us.

In this step, you will speak out in your own words the core pieces out of the first three parts of the inner-healing process and thereby "govern with your words."

Here is a basic template for how your declarations Restating your healing process will follow. You will, of course, fill in the blanks with your own words based on your own experiences in this inner-healing process.

"I choose to stop all of the unhealthy flows of _____ (e.g. depression) in my life right now, and to open up the healthy flows of _____ (e.g. peace/joy/hope) in my life right now.

"I choose to disagree from my heart with the lie(s) that _____"
(state the lies you discovered in step one and two)

"Furthermore, I choose to agree from my heart with the Truth that_____"
(state the Truth you discovered in step three)

"I declare that all unhealthy flows of _____ (depression) in my life are stopped right now. I declare that all healthy flows of _____ (peace/joy/love) in my life are opened up right now!

So be it!

Step Five:
Repeat

Repeat this process for each and every unhealthy flow until they are all healed. They are specific wounds that require specific healing. If you had multiple injuries in an accident, you would need to treat each wound to be healed. Stay with it, once they are healed, they should not bother you again. If they do, reach out to a professional or contact our office for expert help.

THE FAMILY
REFORMATION PROJECT

FAMILY LEGACY IDENTITY PROTOCOL

Family Legacy-
Personality Profile Tool
(Free Tool)

NOTE: There are additional tools and reports available for a small fee through our office from The Everything DiSC™ by Wiley* suite of analytics. See the end of this free tool for more information about these leading personality EQ analytical tools for your family.

The purpose of this tool is to provide the family with a free basic process for understanding each family members unique personality type and the implications that come along with it. This tool will help family members explore their own unique design along with others in the family unit. With this expanded knowledge and increased empathy, family members will engage in conversations to better understand, relate, communicate, and empathize with family members.

Step One:

Select a leader (dad or mom) and then gather the family after a great meal in a relaxed environment. This exercise can be done in a face to face manner for best results, or over video app if need be. Have the leader read or share the purpose for the exercise written above.

Step Two:

Review
Leader says, "Your personality is a part of the answer to the question, "Who am I." This Family Personality Profile tool will help us understand personality preferences such as whether you are more:
- Task driven or relationship driven
- Face or slow paced
- Extroverted or introverted energy
- Methodical or spontaneous
- Precise or innovative
- Challenging or accepting
- Decisive or analytical
- Expressive or contemplative

Leader says, "Our analysis will show us where our predispositions and assumptions are, our blind spots, along with those of other family members. The benefit is that we can then choose to know and respect the design of every individual and use this information to improve our family relationships."

CULTURAL ARCHITECTS

Step Three:

Explore the DISC Diagram

Leader reads through entire diagram and helps members identify where they fit on it.

The graphic below provides a snapshot of the four basic DiSC® styles.

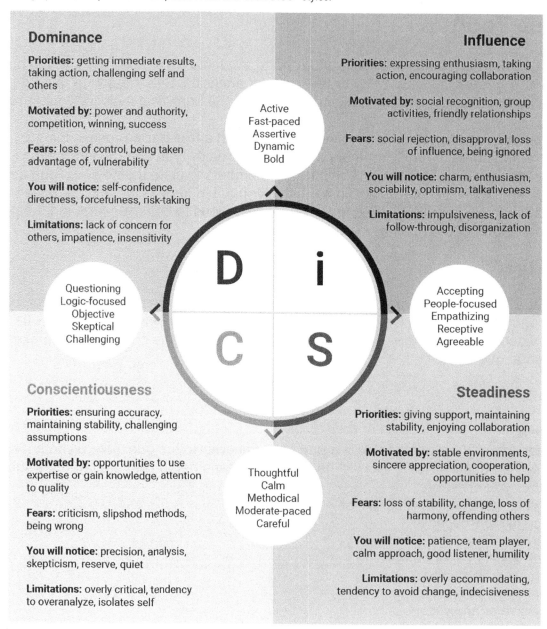

Dominance

Priorities: getting immediate results, taking action, challenging self and others

Motivated by: power and authority, competition, winning, success

Fears: loss of control, being taken advantage of, vulnerability

You will notice: self-confidence, directness, forcefulness, risk-taking

Limitations: lack of concern for others, impatience, insensitivity

Influence

Priorities: expressing enthusiasm, taking action, encouraging collaboration

Motivated by: social recognition, group activities, friendly relationships

Fears: social rejection, disapproval, loss of influence, being ignored

You will notice: charm, enthusiasm, sociability, optimism, talkativeness

Limitations: impulsiveness, lack of follow-through, disorganization

Active
Fast-paced
Assertive
Dynamic
Bold

Questioning
Logic-focused
Objective
Skeptical
Challenging

Accepting
People-focused
Empathizing
Receptive
Agreeable

Conscientiousness

Priorities: ensuring accuracy, maintaining stability, challenging assumptions

Motivated by: opportunities to use expertise or gain knowledge, attention to quality

Fears: criticism, slipshod methods, being wrong

You will notice: precision, analysis, skepticism, reserve, quiet

Limitations: overly critical, tendency to overanalyze, isolates self

Steadiness

Priorities: giving support, maintaining stability, enjoying collaboration

Motivated by: stable environments, sincere appreciation, cooperation, opportunities to help

Fears: loss of stability, change, loss of harmony, offending others

You will notice: patience, team player, calm approach, good listener, humility

Limitations: overly accommodating, tendency to avoid change, indecisiveness

Thoughtful
Calm
Methodical
Moderate-paced
Careful

EVERYTHING **DiSC**
WORKPLACE®

Leader makes copies of the diagram and gives one to everyone as a handout and says, "Let's read one section at a time and identify which family members fit in each one. D – I – S – C"

Copyright ©2021 Revised Edition. The Family Legacy and Cultural Architects. All rights reserved.

CULTURAL ARCHITECTS

Step Three: continued

Leader says, "As we cover each section, draw a dot for each person in the section you think best describes them. One dot per person in the section that best describes them. Include one for yourself. Write the initials of the person beside their dot."

Have Fun!

Step Four:

Debrief and Learning

Leader bring everyone back together and say, "Let's talk about what we learned by everyone joining me is a discussion that addresses a few key questions one at a time."

1. What did you learn about yourself from the diagram? (allow for everyone to answer)
2. What did you learn about others from the diagram? (allow everyone to share their answers)
3. How does what you learned connect to the character qualities, core values, and purpose in our family identity? (allow for everyone to share their answers)
4. What can you do to better connect, communicate, and understand other family members based on what you learned? (allow for everyone to share their answers)
5. How does all of this connect to our family Legacy? (allow for everyone to share their connections)

Step Five:

Application:
Leader says, "Given all that we have learned, how are each of us going to apply the learning in specific ways in the future?" (allow everyone to share their commitments to action

End

*Everything Disc Workplace Profile™ by Wiley

The Everything DiSC Workplace Profile and Comparison Reports from Wiley Publishers are one of many EQ tools available through our office. They are inexpensive and extremely helpful. Contact our office if you would like more information.

Create more effective and productive family relationships
Uses: Team building, communication, conflict management, motivation, productivity, personal development, empathy.

CULTURAL ARCHITECTS

*Everything Disc Workplace Profile™ by Wiley (continued)

It's not just about me; it's about our relationships.
- Gain insights into your own behavior and that of others.
- Understand and appreciate the styles of the people you work with.
- Learn how to make communication more effective.
- Create strategies for overcoming challenges when working with people of different DiSC® styles.

Features of the Workplace Profile (transferable to a family context)
- Profile is for one person.
- Appropriate for ANYONE 12 and over
- 20-page workplace-specific report that focuses on your priorities and strengths as well as those of others. (transferable to a family context)
- Provides clear strategies for building more effective relationships.
- The language of the narrative is supportive, personalized and easily understood without the intervention of an assessment professional.
- Takes 15-20 minutes to complete the survey. Assessment results are available upon completion.

This tool will create one-on-one personality comparisons between pairings of all family members with insights and recommendations for improving each relationship.

$60*   **Per person and includes both individual profile and Comparison Reports**
$275*   **Per person - Profile + 2 -1-hour group coaching calls (unlimited number of people)**
$425*   **Profile + 2 -1-hour personal Coaching calls (one person)**

Contact our office if you would like more information

FAMILY LEGACY IDENTITY PROTOCOL

Family Legacy-
Family Identity CVP Tool
(Character, Values, Purpose)

The purpose of this tool is to provide the family with a process for gaining clarity and insight into the family identity and the family legacy. Through a fun and simple look into all of the data generated in the first six exercises of the identity protocol we will distill it down to:

- the primary family character qualities
- the 8-10 most important family core values
- the purpose for your family

Step One:

Select a leader (dad or mom) and then gather the family after a great meal in a relaxed environment. This exercise can be done in a face to face manner for best results, or over video app if need be. Have the leader read or share the purpose for the exercise written above.

Step Two:

Review:
Leader says, **"The Family Identity CVP Tool** (**C**haracteristics, **V**alues, **P**urpose) will guide your family through a series of questions. Once you've answered and prioritized the results, you will have panned out the gold nuggets and found the family treasure of FAMILY IDENTITY.

This experience leaves most families with:

- An emotional moment together
- Clarity of identity and purpose
- A gratitude for the gifts they carry
- A sense of responsibility to steward this identity
- A desire to live up to the identity and legacy they've received
- An appreciation for one another
- A desire to support the family in living this identity
- A commitment to pass on this legacy

CULTURAL ARCHITECTS

Step Three:

Instructions:
Leader says, "In a moment, we are going to have a discussion and answer a set of questions together as we address all of the family identity work we've done so far."

Leader turns to a clean sheet of flip chart paper and a marker where they will write down the responses from the family to the following questions.
Leader writes "Family Character Qualities" at the very top of the paper.

Step Four:

Questions:
Leader says, "Question number one, question, as we think about all of the identity exercises that we have done so far what character qualities stand out the most for our family and family line?" (make a list and fill the page with responses from family members, keep asking, "what else?" until the sheet is full and people are quiet.

Leader turns to another clean flip chart page of paper and writes at the top, "Family Values"

Leader says, "Question number two, question, as we think about all of the identity exercises that we have done so far, what 8-10 values stand out the most for our family and family line?" (make a list and fill the page with responses from family members, keep asking, "what else?" until the sheet is full and people are quiet. "Values are another way of saying, what are the most important things to our family and family line?"

Leader- Once there are 8-10 core values on the paper the Leader says, "Now we are going to rank these values from the most important one to the next, to the next and so on. The most important value receives the number 1, the next receives the number 2 and so on. Every value is important or it wouldn't be on the paper, but rank them 1-8/10."

Leader turns to another clean flip chart page of paper and writes at the top, "Family Purpose."

Leader says, "Question number three, question, as we think about all of the identity exercises that we have done so far what do you think the purpose for our family and family line is, and why?" (listen carefully making sure everyone has a chance to respond, draw out of the various ideas about the family purpose)

Leader works with the family to craft a short phrase or sentence about the family purpose based on responses. Leader writes it down on the paper and asks for additional clarification until there is agreement from the family.

CULTURAL ARCHITECTS

Step Five:

Debrief and Learning:
Leader bring everyone back together and say, "Let's talk about what we learned by everyone joining me in a discussion that addresses a few key questions one at a time."

1. What are the top 10 family character qualities that best describe us? (allow for everyone to share their answers)

Family Identity CVP Tool (Character, Values, Purpose)
Step Five: continued
Debrief and Learning

2. What are the top 8-10 family values in order of importance and why? (allow for everyone to share their answers)
3. What is our family purpose? Do we all agree? (allow for everyone to share their answers)

Insight:

The work to this point in the identity protocol is meant to give clarity and buy in to the true identity of the family and the family line. This is the true identity and true legacy of the family. This is a powerful moment. Treat this exercise and this moment with your family with the sincerity and honor it deserves, together

Step Six:

Application:
Leader says, "How does it feel to know who we are?" "How will knowing this effect how we do life day to day as a family? (allow time for everyone to respond)

Leader, save the flip chart papers filled up with writing as you will need them in the Coat of Arms Exercise.

FAMILY LEGACY IDENTITY PROTOCOL

Family Legacy-
Family Coat of Arms Tool

THE FAMILY
REFORMATION PROJECT

The purpose of this tool is to provide a process for the family to deeply connect emotionally to each other and to the family identity while creating a one of a kind, work of art together in the form of a family Coat of Arms.

Step One:

Select a leader (dad or mom and then gather the family after a great meal in a relaxed environment. This exercise can be done in a face to face manner for best results, or over video app if need be. Have the leader read or share the purpose for the exercise written above. All of the previous Identity Protocol exercises must be completed prior to doing the Family Coat of Arms, process matters.

Step Two:

Instructions:
Leader says, "In a moment we are going to engage in a powerful experience of affirming the identity and character of each and every family member one at a time. The entire family will declare characteristics they experience of each family member as **they write what they hear on a flip chart paper.** When they are complete and the paper is filled, they entire family will celebrate each and every member one at a time. It's glorious!"

Leader says, "Once everyone has had their turn, a new creative process begins. We will follow a process of taking all of the information from all 8 identity exercises and fashion them into a work of art for the ages! Our very own Family Coat of Arms. As you learn how to do this process, you will know how to do this with your own families someday."

Leader says, "If a picture is worth a thousand words, our family coat of arms and its 10-15 images is declaring a narrative about our family identity and legacy of more than 10,000 words at a glance. Let's get started!

CULTURAL ARCHITECTS

Step Three:

Exercise

Leader says, "Everyone form a huge circle. Who is going to be the first person to go?" (Hand them the marker and set them beside a clean flip chart paper; have them write their name across the top of the paper)

Leader says, "Each person will have a turn to hear from those who know them best, what are the character qualities that you see and experience of that individual, who are they to you? Each person will have 5-10 minutes to write down the specific character qualities being shared on the paper."

Leader says, "Here are a few important guidelines to follow in sharing affirmations:
- Be kind
- Be positive
- Be encouraging
- Be focused in your comments, don't ramble or dominate
- Let everyone speak
- Speak to the character qualities of each person (kind, loving, courageous, creative, humble, etc.)"

Leader says, "Here we go! What are the character qualities that you experience in *name here*? Begin!

Leader make sure everyone shares and that the individual hears the comments and writes them up on the paper with small to medium size writing to accommodate a lot of input. Keep drawing out positive characteristics until the sheet is full and the person is adequately affirmed.

Leader says, "Ok, that's it for now! Everyone gather around *name* and smother them with a big family group hug!" I encourage you as the leader to start a name chant and while everyone is in the big family group hug start chanting, "*name, name, name, name, name!* "

NOTE:
This is an important part of the experience and it will create a lasting and meaningful emotional imprint on the person receiving the affirmations and being celebrated by the family!

Leader says, "OK, tear off the page and stick it up on the wall so that there is a fresh page of flip chart paper for the next person to use. Who is next?"

Repeat this process for every person in the family. Make sure to fill the paper and to celebrate each person with a group hug and name chant. Have Fun! Do not allow any criticism, sarcasm, or negative comments

CULTURAL ARCHITECTS

Step Four:

Identify Top 10
Once everyone is complete, identify the 10 most common characteristics present on all of the individual affirmation charts. List them below, only 10.

Leader says, "Looking at all of our papers, Let's identify the 10-character qualities most common to all of us and **write them on a new blank sheet of paper**." The 10 most common that appear on all of the individual sheets into one list of those 10. (do it

   1
   2
   3
   4
   5
   6
   7
   8
   9
  10

Step Five:

Family True Identity
Leader says, "Over the next hour or so, we are going to glean from all 8 of the identity exercises a total of 15 of the top family character qualities, core values, and purpose to consolidate all of the research into our family true identity. Then we will fashion them into our family Coat of Arms!"

NOTE:
Leader – you are working to identify 15 words that best describe your family true identity based on all 8 identity exercises. Review the exercises to distill down a list.

True Identity
Family History
Family Genetic History
Family Generational History
Inner Healing
Family Personality Profile * (This tool and reports are only available for a small fee)
Family Identity CVP (Character, Values, Purpose)
Family Coat of Arms

CULTURAL ARCHITECTS

Step Five: (continued)

Family True Identity

Once again, from all of the research, identify the following
- List of 15 words that describe family character, values, and purpose
- A short family purpose motto or statement of a few words

Instructions:

Leader- once you have your list of 15 and the family purpose motto or statement you have what you need to begin work creating the Family Coat of Arms. The leader will lead a discussion walking you through the process step by step.

Exercise:

Leader says, "We are going to create a Family Coat of Arms (COA) by first having a discussion addressing several key questions."

Leader says, "On a clean sheet of flip chart paper, lets brainstorm possible images or symbols that represent each one of our 15 family true identity words. We will eventually work these into the COA." (allow enough time for everyone to input into each of the words) Leader- write or draw the images/symbols on the paper. E.g. leadership may have image ideas of eagle, lion, or a compass; courage may have image ideas like lion, bear, etc.

Leader says, "Now that we have image ideas for all of the family true identity words, lets assign one image to each of the words now and make a final image list 1-15 on a clean sheet of flip chart paper."

1	2	3	4	5
6	7	8	9	10
11	12	13	14	15

Leader says, "Here are the images we will work into the Family COA!"

Leader says, "Next, we need to make a final decision about our family purpose motto or purpose description. What have we come up with so far? Does anyone have any other suggestions?" Leader write down options and vote to determine a motto.

Exercise:

Leader says, "There are several more key decisions to be made as we move into the design phase of the family COA including:
- Shape of the shield
- Supporters of the sides of the shield (yes/no/what)
- Placement of images on shield, above, below, behind,
- Writing on the edge of the shield or not
- 1 or 2 banners at the top, bottom, or both

Step Five: (continued)

Designing the Family Coat of Arms
- Shape of the banners
- Motto and name placement on banners
- Colors
- Fonts
- Sizes
- More..."

Leader facilitate a discussion with family members to gain agreement on the specific items of the COA. Select the artists of the family and commission them to put the work you've done into a sketch or computer image and go from there.

The Bixby Coat of Arms

NOTE:
We realize that you may or may not be a family with creatives and artists to bring this piece of art across the finish line. If you have the skill set in your family to produce a finished piece, have at it! If, on the other hand, you want some help with design through to final production, we are here to help. ***Contact our office and we will put you in touch with our preferred vendors who can work with you to produce a family coat of arms that is meaningful and enduring***

Once you have this finished family identity art piece, the Family Coat of Arms, it becomes a priceless tool for:
- Communicating the family identity, character, values, and purpose to generation after generation
- Stories and conversations around the table and in the practice of the other Family Legacy Protocols
- Coaching conversations and personal development plans
- True Identity" gear, the creation of unique products and services using your family coat of arms
- Passing on your family legacy effectively, powerfully and visually.

Family Coat of Arms Tool (continued)

There are two other significant "Family Identity" pieces of art I want to recommend to you. Both of these reinforce the family identity but in a very personal and unique way.

The Family Painting
The Family Song

Both of these Family Identity pieces are done exclusively by my daughter and son-in-love under the ministry business of "Cultural Artisans". They are also our preferred vendor for the creation of the digital Family Coat of Arms.

They are gifted musicians and artists who will take you through a process and create for your family a true original and one of a kind Family Painting and Family Song that speak to your family true identity and family purpose.

If you are interested in any one of the three pieces mentioned above, please contact our office and we will get the process going.

THE FAMILY
REFORMATION PROJECT

FAMILY LEGACY IDENTITY PROTOCOL

Family Legacy-
Rule 51 Tool for Revelation

The purpose of this tool is to provide the family with a process to receive a revelation around your individual and family true identity, purpose and legacy. It is important to note that the tool I'm going to share with you will work to bring you revelation on *any matter* you seek deeper wisdom, knowledge, and understanding on.

Step One:

Select a leader (dad or mom and then gather the family after a great meal in a relaxed environment. This exercise can be done in a face to face manner for best results, or over video app if need be. Have the leader read or share the purpose for the exercise written above.

Step Two:

Review:
Leader says, "This exercise and tool are called, "Rule 51." It's named Rule 51 for this reason, It serves as a reminder to spend the majority of your personal prayer and meditation time listening instead of talking. It is a commitment to listen 51% or more of my time in prayer, a majority of time spent. That's it. Learning to ask a few good questions and then cultivate our own "ears to hear" what God is thinking, saying or doing in relation to the question. It is this ability to listen or to "hear" that is the secret to experiencing a revelation.

Leader says, "In a moment the Rule 51 Tool will walk you through three questions that you can ask of the Lord every day. As you write in a journaling style what you sense and hear Him saying in response to your questions, you will receive revelation wisdom, knowledge, and instruction. It is the skill of learning to have "ears to hear what the Spirit of God is saying" that is the skill of receiving revelation."

Step Three:

Exercise:
Leader says, "We are going to learn this tool by using it together right now. The plan is for each of us to begin to use this tool on a regular or even a daily basis to grow our skill at having "ears that hear" and grow in our ability to receive revelation knowledge as a result."

CULTURAL ᴀRCHITECTS

Step Three: (continued)

Exercise:
Leader says, **"First, everyone take out a pen and notebook, journal, or a few pieces of paper.** I will give us three questions, one at a time. After each question, we will take five minutes to write out our answer using a specific technique which I will show to you in a moment."

Leader says, "Write this question down on your paper. Question number one, question, "Father, what do You want me to know about You today? Next, just below that question write, "*your name*, I want you to know that, _____ continue writing what you hear, see, or sense and write in the voice of God speaking directly to you. Write."

Leader says, "Write this question down on your paper. Question number two, question, "Father, what do You want me to know about Me today? Next, just below that question write, "*your name*, I want you to know that, _____ continue writing what you hear, see, or sense and write in the voice of God speaking directly to you. Write."

Leader says, "Write this question down on your paper. Question number three, question, "Father, what do You want me to know about _____ today? Write in the blank any single question or issue that you want revelation on. E.g. my purpose, or my identity, or our family purpose, or a specific decision that needs to be made,   ONE THING in the blank. Next, just below that question write, "*your name*, I want you to know that, _____ continue writing what you hear, see, or sense and write in the voice of God speaking directly to you. Write."

NOTE: For the purpose of learning how to use this tool, give everyone five minutes to write after each question. Of course, everyone can take as much time as they want to when they are on their own. It is also very important that you choose to believe that God is speaking to you when you ask Him your questions and write down what you are hearing. If you ask with doubt, don't expect to receive any revelation. Believe.

Step Four:

Debrief and Learning:
Leader bring everyone back together and say, "Let's talk about what we learned by everyone joining me is a discussion that addresses a few key questions one at a time."
1. What did you learn about Father today? (allow for everyone to share their answers)
2. What did you learn about you today (allow for everyone to share their answers)
3. What did you learn about the issue you wrote in the blank for question 3? (allow for everyone to share their answers)
4. What did you learn about listening and hearing God? allow for everyone to share their connections)
5. How is what you heard and learned connected to our family Legacy? (allow for everyone to share their connections)

Step Five:

Application:
Leader says, "Given all that we have learned, we are each going to apply the learning in a specific way now and in the future."

Leader says, "This is a very simple process. So simple that you may be tempted to dismiss its power to deliver life changing epiphanies and revelation. The choice is yours; it always is. I would encourage you to use the tool for thirty days and then judge for yourself the value you are receiving from its use. If you don't experience deeper revelation knowledge in the matter of your inquiry, something is amiss. I have only seen this tool work 100% of the time when used as directed. Reach out to our office or website for help using this and other tools."

CULTURAL ᴧRCHITECTS

FAMILY LEGACY IDENTITY PROTOCOL

Choice to Believe Identity Tool

THE FAMILY
REFORMATION PROJECT

The purpose of this tool is to provide the family with an opportunity to live their legacy to the full by starting with a fresh choice to *believe.* The choice to agree with the true identity that the identity exercises have uncovered along with the choice to agree with the revelation that they received in Rule 51, will shift things profoundly. "For as He thinks in his heart, so is he." Proverbs 23:7 (NKJV) In other words, we create the life experiences that we agree with from the heart. Belief or faith is a key to living life in agreement with your identity and your legacy.

Step One:

Select a leader (dad or mom) and then gather the family after a great meal in a relaxed environment. This exercise can be done in a face to face manner for best results, or over video app if need be. Have the leader read or share the purpose for the exercise written above.

Step Two:

Exercise:
Leader say, "The simplicity and power of the choice to believe cannot be overstated. By design, belief (faith, choice to agree with God) is the currency of heaven. We receive all of heavens benefits by faith. Period."

Leader says, "And so it is when it comes to believing in our family design, family true identity, and individual identity, purpose and so on."

Leader says, "Given all of our research, seeking, and listening, it is now time to make a decision both individually and as a family. I have four questions for each of us. I will read them one at a time and then I'll ask each of you to offer a simple verbal yes or no to indicate your choice of agreement."

Leader says,
First, do you choose to agree with our family true identity?	Yes	No
Second, do you choose to agree with your individual true identity?	Yes	No
Third, do you choose to agree with our family purpose?	Yes	No
Fourth, do you choose to agree with your individual purpose?	Yes	No

Do not over complicate this and do not underestimate the power of belief. You will create what you choose to believe, choose wisely.

Step Two: (Continued)

Exercise:
If you made the choice to believe, then it's time to start making other choices and taking other actions as a result of your faith in your identity and purpose. Setting goals and having the support of a coach to go after those goals is an important next step.

Debrief and Learning: Discuss what you learned from this simple tool?

FAMILY LEGACY IDENTITY PROTOCOL

Family Legacy-
Coach Approach Tool

THE FAMILY
REFORMATION PROJECT

The purpose of this tool is to equip the family with a coaching conversation process that will empower family members to live from a place of true identity and family legacy. The coach approach will empower the family to self-govern well and steward the family as designed.

Step One:

Select a leader (dad or mom) and then gather the family after a great meal in a relaxed environment. This exercise can be done in a face to face manner for best results, or over video app if need be. Have the leader read or share the purpose for the exercise written above.

Step Two:

Review:
This tool will equip the family with a simple coach approach conversation tool that can be used to support family members in consistently demonstrating their identity, purpose, and legacy. It will serve as a guide for specific and measurable actions that bring growth and maturity to how members show up in day to day life. Over time and with consistent practice, the coach approach will produce meaningful results.

For example, if a family has creativity, leadership, and loyalty as three of their core characteristics, the coach approach would support each member in determining:
- the short- and long-term goals they set to live in alignment with these characteristics
- the specific actions to take in the next 30 days to show up as a loyal and creative leader at work, at home, and in life
- the lessons they are learning and how they are growing in creativity, leadership, and loyalty over the past 30 days
- how to make decisions in life through the lenses of loyalty, creativity and leadership

As in the other protocols, the coach approach is an intentional process of:
- goal setting
- measurable action
- curiosity and exploration
- asking good questions
- empathetic listening
- a partnership in problem solving
- learning
- support

Step Two: (continued

Review:
The Family Legacy Coach approach Tool will guide you through a simple coaching conversation model that you can use with your family in multiple context and for a variety of outcomes. It is indispensable as a mechanism for growth and stewardship.

A frequency of even one coaching conversation per month with each family member will change the trajectory of the family legacy. Furthermore, it will teach our children how to embody the family identity and steward the family legacy for generations to come. This is an inside-out process that will transform our families, businesses, communities and culture.

The Coach Approach
Another key distinction of the Family Legacy Model *is integrating The Coach Approach into the context of the family.* The dynamic of family relationships are transformed when we intentionally partner with family members in a proven practice that supports one another in discovery, growth, and success. Imagine experiencing your family as a primary place of resource in your growth and success. For many, this is beyond their ability to imagine. For others, the concept is familiar, but the step by step process in unclear.

Coaching is one of the most empowering and invigorating modalities in creating growth and success offered today. To integrate this into the Family Legacy Model by investing into the personal growth and development of each member is a powerful way to do family. Family coaching is an effective way to build legacy while training our children how to bring coaching into their generations to come.

If you want to ensure the best outcome as you apply the Family Legacy Model™, you simply must understand how to facilitate supportive family coaching conversations effectively. Coaching conversations are distinct from conversations where you "give advice" or where you say, "Let me tell how to do this and what I have done when in your situation." That is more of a mentoring conversation. There is a time and a place for different conversations, no doubt, but the conversation that causes safety, support, growth and personal responsibility, is the coaching conversation.

Good coaching is a dynamic partnership between coach and coachee in a simple and creative process to maximize the coachee's personal and professional potential. It is a growth conversation that can address any aspect of life from relationships, to career, to health, and spiritual growth. A true coaching conversation is one that the coach asks a few good questions and listens while the coachee finds their own answers to the questions. Once they have their own "aha" moment, they are supported in taking personal responsibility and choosing what's important, what is the learning, and what they will do next in the pursuit of a clear and meaningful goal.

Step Two: (continued)

Review:
As you plan for the coaching conversations specifically designed in the protocols along with having coaching conversations in everyday life informally, you may want to review this section to keep your skills sharp. In addition, I have a digital E-Course on the Website entitled The Coach Approach to Family that will equip you in a detailed manner in learning a coach approach.

The Basics of a Coach Approach

Goal Setting
Effective coaching conversations are anchored by a clear, measurable, and meaningful goal that a family member is working to achieve. The goal can be focused on any area or topic of their life that they authentically care about improving, changing or creating new. Any area that they want support in making happen can be made into a specific and measurable goal.

For example:
- In the next 30 days, I choose to decide on what career field to go into.
- By the end of the month I choose to loose 5 lbs and to eat healthy.
- In the next 90 days I choose to make a job transition.
- This week I choose to get an A on my upcoming math test.
- This month I choose to get all of any house chores done on time.
- In the next 30 days I choose to work and save $300 for a new billiards table for the family.
- This year I choose to save $5,000 to take the family on a Family Legacy Venture trip to Florida.
- I choose to determine my core values and work on time mastery over the next 90 days.

Here are a list of topics and areas for everyone to consider when choosing a possible goal to work towards with the support of the family.

Potential Coaching Topics
- What am I tolerating that I really want to be different in my life? What exactly does "different" look like?
- What area of my life do I specifically want to improve over the next 30 days?
- Health, faith, school, job, finances, fun, relationships, energy level, time mastery, serving others
- Where am I experiencing conflict in my life and how do I resolve it in the next week?
- What areas of my life, skills, character, career etc. do I want to grow in over the next 90 days?

Step Two: (continued)

Review:
- What challenges am I facing that I want to overcome in the next period of time?
- What projects do I want to complete at home, work or school in the next 30 days?
- What relationships need to be fixed, healed, stopped or changed over the next period of time?
- What problems am I facing that need to be solved in the next time period?
- What opportunities are in front of me and how will I decide what to do?

Each family member decides for themselves what exactly they want to be coached on. Once they have set a clear, measurable and meaningful goal it's time for the coaching conversation.

The Coaching Conversation

Coaching conversations can happen anytime between family members and are a true gift to each other. However, during the regular Family Legacy Model™ protocols, brief and focused coaching conversations that occur one person at a time for 5-10 minutes each, as time permits are so valuable.

Here are the five simple questions for the coach (leader) to ask…
What's Important to you today? (Current goal)
What are the challenges and possible solutions?
What are you learning?
What will you do before our next ritual?
How can we help?

Nearly all of the talking that happens in a coaching conversation is done by the person being coached (coachee). The coach only asks the 5 questions while everyone else listens quietly. Very brief advising may be helpful if the coachee is stuck. As a rule the coach speaks 20% of the time and the coachee speaks 80% of the time.
So much more can be learned about how to be a more effective coach. I enjoy training coaches as much as anything else I get to do. However, keep it simple for best results. Don't overcomplicate things. Don't solve the coachees problems for them. Help them solve them for themselves. You will be glad you did when you see them grow before your very eyes.

Step Two: (continued)

Additional important guidelines for successful coaching conversations
- Be a great listener not an advisor, teller, lecturer etc. Be quick to listen and slow to speak as a coach.
- Don't push your own agenda. Allow the coachee to own their own process, decisions, and actions.
- Be curious and use your limited 20% talk time to ask a few good questions. Explore
- Keep the environment safe. Do not allow criticism, sarcasm, cutting remarks by anyone.
- Keep it simple. Follow the Five coaching questions listed above.
- Make sure there are clear and measurable goals to start with and actions to end with each coaching conversation.
- Stay positive and supportive through the entire coaching conversation.

Step Three:

Exercise:
Practice coaching conversations with your family members by using the following tool often. To use the approach to grow in character, values and purpose as uncovered in the identity protocols, simple put one of these into the first question of What is important for you today? E.g. to grow in leadership or integrity in the next 30 days.

Once the (growth) goal is set, the conversation should run smoothly and be very supportive in partnering with your family member to achieve their goal. Nice work coach!

Coaching conversation once again for your easy reference:

Here are the five simple questions for the coach (leader) to ask...
What's Important to you today? (Current goal)
What are the challenges and possible solutions?
What are you learning?
What will you do before our next ritual?
How can we help?

If you would like support in developing your coaching skills, please visit our website or call our office. We have a number of tools, e-courses, webinars, workshops and coaching services to help you grow.

FAMILY LEGACY RITUAL PROTOCOL

Family Legacy-
Ritual Protocol 3

THE FAMILY
REFORMATION PROJECT

The purpose of The Family Legacy Ritual Protocol™ is to equip the family to engage in a regular intentional family meeting that makes doing family together life giving, supportive, purposeful and fun while empowering the entire family to succeed. It is a loosely structured gathering where families build memories, learn lessons, share life, and honor God as appropriate to each unique family dynamic.

The Family Ritual is the "meat and potatoes" of the week to week journey of living a lasting legacy. The protocol is somewhat reflective of the Shabbat practice of the Israelis. The consistent rhythm of gathering together as a family to enjoy rituals in a framework of delicious food and sharing stories, listening and learning, laughing and crying while having fun and supporting each other in life's journey with a basic coach approach is a profoundly impactful practice.

The Designer, in His wisdom, purposed a regular weekly family meeting where there was a stoppage from work and a set of rituals for the good and blessing of the family.

*"Those who find true wisdom **obtain tools** for **understanding** the proper way to live, for they will have a **fountain of blessing pouring** into their lives..."*
Proverbs 3:13 TPT

Definition
The Family Legacy Ritual Protocol™ is the weekly/regular family meeting that empowers your family to succeed by intentionally engaging each other over delicious food, great fun, interesting stories, timeless wisdom, and a supportive coach approach.

A ritual is any practice or pattern of behavior regularly practiced in a set manner. What do I mean by "regular"? The Biblical idea of regular in this context seems to suggest once a week and would certainly produce a lot of fruit at that frequency. If not weekly, then how often should the rituals be practiced ensuring a full blessing?

That's up to each family to decide based on their own set of circumstances and the outcomes they are committed to. Every other week is a good frequency and will produce solid results. At a minimum, once a month is necessary to gain the benefit of the protocol.

The intentional engagement of your family through this practice will result in deep and profound growth of character, intimacy between family members, the development of next generation leaders and culture shapers, the creating and transfer of the family legacy, and your children being equipped to repeat this protocol for generations to come.

The Family Legacy Ritual Protocol™ *framework* is a simple, yet profound set of practices that never grow old. There are endless combinations of foods to eat, games to play, cat videos to watch, life stories to tell, subjects to cover, questions to ask, goals to go after and prayers to pray etc.

The Family Legacy Ritual Protocol™ Framework
- Planning
- Focus
- Food
- Story
- Coaching
- Wisdom
- FUN
- Clean up

I've often said that, "The wisdom of God is cloaked in *simplicity*." My experience has been consistent with the scripture where it states that, "…He hides things from the wise and learned and reveals them to babes." (the simple) How many times in our journeys of faith do we over complicate things and miss all together the ease, wisdom and effectiveness of simplicity? Simple obedience to prescribed protocols that sustain a legacy for generations though the testing, trials and travesties the Jews have endured should be all of the proof we need to grasp the magnitude of this protocol.

A weekly, or at least a regular, family gathering where there is a simple set of practices that build the family in a myriad of vitally important ways is brilliant! Only a master Designer could accomplish so much with so little.

It is so simple to do… and so simple not to do

CULTURAL ARCHITECTS

THE FAMILY
REFORMATION PROJECT

FAMILY LEGACY FAMILY RITUAL PROTOCOL

Family Ritual-
Launch Gathering

The first exercise in the Family Legacy Ritual Protocol™ is the Family Ritual Launch Gathering. When it's time to introduce the family to your decision to begin having regular Family Ritual meetings, gather everyone together for a Ritual Launch Gathering. In this gathering you will introduce the purpose and framework of the of the Family Ritual Protocol. You will complete the Family Ritual Launch Tool™ together to build the interest and commitment of family members by including them in the planning process. You may have heard it said that without "weigh in" there is no "buy in". From the beginning of this protocol it's important to involve everyone in the process of formulating your unique Family Ritual.

Family Ritual Launch Tool™

In preparation for the gathering:
Who is going to facilitate or lead your family Launch Gathering?

What are the gathering details?

Date	Time	Location

Who is invited?

Send invites.

1. Gather resources needed for the Launch Gathering-
   - Snacks
   - Flip chart and markers or
   - Worksheets

2. Review the Ritual purpose, definition, framework, and tips Pray about the launch.

CULTURAL /\RCHITECTS

3. The Gathering:

- The leader calls the Family Ritual Gathering officially to order. (Turn off cell phones, computers, electronics)
- The leader shares from the heart (or reading) the purpose, definition and framework of this protocol.

Purpose- The purpose of The Family Legacy Ritual Protocol™ is to equip the family to engage in a regular intentional family meeting that makes doing family together life giving, supportive, purposeful and fun while empowering the entire family to succeed. It is a loosely structured gathering where families build memories, learn lessons, share life, and honor God as appropriate to each unique family dynamic.

Definition- The Family Legacy Ritual Protocol™ is the weekly/regular family meeting that empowers your family to succeed by intentionally engaging each other over delicious food, great fun, interesting stories, and a supportive coach approach ritual.

Framework of the weekly/regular Family Ritual Meeting
- Food
- Story
- Coaching
- Wisdom
- FUN
- Clean up

4. The leader explains that the Launch Gathering is to get everyone's help and input for the Rituals. In addition, everyone will have ritual responsibilities of some kind including food prep, talking, listening, playing games and cleaning up. The Family Ritual Meetings are not a spectator event, everyone gets to engage

5. With a flip chart up on the wall and a marker the leader begins to gather everyones input.

6. The leader proposes a time, place and frequency of upcoming Ritual meetings and gets agreement. Then writes up on the flip chart the details of the agreement.

7. The leader lets everyone know that you are planning for about 3 months of Ritual Meetings at this time. Somewhere between 3 and 13 meetings depending on frequency.

8. The leader writes "FOOD" up on the flip chart and asks everyone for favorite meal suggestions that will become the menu for the family rituals. After getting a page of ideas. Narrow it down and vote so that you set a basic menu. Have fun!Make sure to get everyone's input.

9. The Leader writes "Story Topics" at the top of a blank flip chart page and shares that at each ritual meeting, everyone will share a brief story (3 minutes) with the family. Ask for everyone's help in brainstorming a list of possible topics. Write down the responses. Remember to guide the suggestions towards important and valuable legacy kinds of topics. See the Ritual Idea Tool™ for guidance. Selecting meaningful topics is a key to bringing increasing value to the family. Once ideas are written down, let everyone know you will pick from the list moving forward. Have fun! Again, make sure to get every   one's input.

10. The leader writes "Coaching" on the top of a blank flip chart page and shares how as a family we want to be supportive of each other's dreams and goals and help each other reach them. At each ritual meeting, everyone will have a chance bring up one of their goals and answer 5 simple questions that will help them in making it happen.

11. The leader then writes the questions below while talking about them.
"The 5 questions are:
What's Important to you? (Current goal)
What are the challenges and possible solutions?
What are you learning?
What will you do before our next ritual?
How can we help?"

12. The leader then asks everyone to share some of the goals they might be thinking about. Make it fun! Make it meaningful. Encourage them if they get stuck by suggesting. What about health, grades, faith, sports, career choice or project completion for example. Assure everyone that this is a safe and positive, supportive experience.

13. The leader writes "Wisdom" on the top of a flip chart page and explains that the family ritual meeting will also have a section where the family will read a scripture and or pray together. The leader can ask if there are any ideas of scriptures or topics from the Bible that they have an interest in exploring and write down responses on the paper. Inform everyone that you will be making choices from the suggestions.

14. The leader writes "FUN" on the top of a flip chart page and explains that the family ritual meeting will also include a fun family activity. Ask for suggestions of fun activities and write them down on the paper. Make sure you hear from everyone.

15. The leader writes "Clean Up" on the top of a flip chart page and explains that everyone gets to help clean up.

16. When you've gathered all the input and the paper is all over the walls let everyone know how fun and exciting this is going to be!

17. Thank everyone for their input and finalize your Gathering by making all of the choices for the first official Family Ritual Meeting and remind everyone of the date, time, place etc.

18. Determine what the first family ritual will be.
Ritual Food
Ritual Story Topic
Ritual Coaching Goal (each individual)
Ritual Wisdom Topic
Ritual FUN Activity
Ritual Clean up All in

19. The leader officially closes the Launch Gathering. This is a great time to share your heart around family and legacy. It is also a great time to pray and ask for God's guidance and blessing on your family ritual meetings.

You now have a great deal of input from the family and it should be easy to plan out the family ritual meetings for at least 3 months. By doing it this way, you have also engaged everyone in the process and gotten greater buy in from members to show up

THE FAMILY
REFORMATION PROJECT

FAMILY LEGACY FAMILY RITUAL PROTOCOL

Family Ritual-
Agenda Exercise

In order to maximize the focus and intentionality of each Family Ritual Meeting, it is helpful to have an agenda to follow. It is important for the family ritual meeting to strike a balance between planning and free flow in order to address the topics that will build a healthy family legacy. If you want to end up at a specific location, you need a map. At the same time, once in a while you can do a little exploring along the way.

Planning out the details make it much more likely that each meeting will be executed effectively for the good of everyone and for the family legacy. I've provided a simple tool to plan and distribute to everyone prior to each family ritual meeting so everyone is prepared for their assignments and their contributions.

Family Ritual Agenda Tool™

The Purpose of this tool is to help you plan the details of an individual family ritual meeting and to share it with family participants.

Date	Time	Location

Food
What's for dinner?

Who's doing the grocery shopping?

Who's doing the food preparation, cooking and set up?

Story
What is the story topic?

CULTURAL ARCHITECTS

Coaching
What are the goals members are working on? Name and goal listed here for each member

_____

Five questions for easy reference:
What's Important to you? (Current goal)
What are the challenges and possible solutions?
What are you learning?
What will you do before our next ritual?
How can we help?

Wisdom
What is the wisdom scripture reading?

_____

Who will be praying?

_____

FUN
What is the family fun activity?

_____

Clean Up
What are the assignments for clean up? Who's doing what?

Name- task

_____

Next ritual meeting date and time is

_____

By using this tool, you can plan intentionally and communicate the plan to family members. You will also have a record of your meetings to keep so you can see what you've covered and what is left to cover that is important to your family legacy. In addition, you are leaving a wonderful codified record of how you did family that you can pass on to generations to come to reinforce the practice of the importance of the family ritual meeting.

CULTURAL /\RCHITECTS

FAMILY LEGACY RITUAL PROTOCOL

Family Legacy-
Ritual Advance Planning Tool™

THE FAMILY
REFORMATION PROJECT

Who will be leading the next 3 months of family ritual meetings?

The leader lets everyone know that you are planning for about 3 months of Ritual Meetings at this time. Somewhere between 3 and 13 meetings depending on frequency.

The leader writes "What worked?" at the top of a blank flip chart page and gets feedback from family members on what worked from the last 3 months of ritual meetings. The leader writes them down. Make it fun.

The leader writes "What didn't work?" at the top of a blank flip chart page and gets feedback from family members on what didn't work from the last 3 months of ritual meetings. The leader writes them down. Make it fun.

The leader writes "what did we learn?" at the top of a blank flip chart page and gets feedback from family members on what was learned from the last 3 months of ritual meetings. The leader writes them down. Make it fun. Reflect on valuable responses.

The leader writes "FOOD" up on the flip chart and asks everyone for favorite meal suggestions that will become the menu for the family rituals. After getting a page of ideas. Narrow it down and vote so that you set a basic menu. Have fun! Make sure to get everyone's input.

The Leader writes "Story Topics" Ask for everyone's help in brainstorming a new list of possible topics. Write down the responses. Remember to guide the suggestions towards important and valuable legacy kinds of topics. See the Ritual Idea Tool for guidance. Selecting meaningful topics is a key to bringing increasing value to the family. Once ideas are written down, let everyone know you will pick from the list moving forward. Have fun! Again, make sure to get everyone's input.

The leader writes "Coaching" on the top of a blank flip chart page and shares how as a family we want to be supportive of each other's dreams and goals and help each other reach them.

The leader then asks everyone to share some new goals they might be thinking about. Make it fun! Make it meaningful. Encourage them if they get stuck by suggesting. What about health, grades, faith, sports, career choice or project completion for example. Assure everyone that this is a safe and positive, supportive experience.

Ritual Advance Planning Tool (continued)

The leader writes "Wisdom" on the top of a flip chart page and explains that the family ritual meeting will continue to have a section where the family will read a scripture and or pray together. The leader can ask if there are any new ideas of scriptures or topics from the Bible that they have an interest in exploring and write down responses on the paper.

The leader writes "FUN" on the top of a flip chart page and explains that the family ritual meeting will also include a fun family activity. Ask for new suggestions of fun activities and write them down on the paper. Make sure you hear from everyone.

The leader writes "Clean Up" on the top of a flip chat page and explains that everyone still gets to help clean up. Hahahaha.

FAMILY LEGACY FAMILY RITUAL PROTOCOL

THE FAMILY
REFORMATION PROJECT

Family Ritual-
Coaching Tool™

The purpose of this tool is to help you understand how to facilitate supportive family ritual coaching conversations effectively. Coaching conversations are distinct from conversations where you "give advice" or where you say, "Let me tell you how to do this and what I have done when in your situation." That's more of a mentoring conversation.

Good coaching is a dynamic partnership between coach and coachee in a simple and creative process to maximize the coachee's personal and professional potential. A true coaching conversation is one that the coach asks a few good questions and listens while the coachee finds their own answers to the questions. Once they have their own "aha" moment, they are supported in taking personal responsibility and choosing what's important, what is the learning, and what they will do next in the pursuit of a clear and meaningful goal.

Coaching is one of the most empowering and invigorating modalities in creating growth and success offered today. To bring this into the family ritual and to invest in the personal growth and development of each member is a powerful way to do family. Family coaching is an effective way to build legacy while training our children how to bring coaching into their generations to come.

As you plan for the coaching conversations during the family ritual meetings, periodically review the sections in Chapter 4 entitled:
Getting the most from your family legacy work and
Tips for effectively leading your own Family Legacy Protocols

Goal Setting
Effective coaching conversations are anchored by a clear, measurable, and meaningful goal that a family member is working to achieve. The goal can be focused on any area or topic of their life that they authentically care about improving, changing or creating new. Any area that they want support in making happen can be made into a specific and measurable goal.

For example:
- In the next 30 days, I choose to decide on what career field to go into.
- By the end of the month I choose to lose 5 pounds and to eat healthy.
- In the next 90 days I choose to make a job transition.
- This week I choose to get an A on my upcoming math test.
- This month I choose to get all of any house chores done on time.

CULTURAL ARCHITECTS

- In the next 30 days I choose to work and save $300 for a new billiards table for the family.
- This year I choose to save $5,000 to take the family on a Family Legacy Venture trip to Florida.
- I choose to determine my core values and work on time mastery over the next 90 days.

Here are a list of topics and areas for everyone to consider when choosing a possible goal to work towards with the support of the family.

Topics for potential coaching to consider

- What am I tolerating that I really want to be different in my life? What exactly does "different" look like?
- What area of my life do I specifically want to improve over the next 30 days?
- Health, faith, school, job, finances, fun, relationships, energy level, time mastery, serving others
- Where am I experiencing conflict in my life and how do I resolve it in the next week?
- What areas of my life, skills, character, career etc. do I want to grow in over the next 90 days?
- What challenges am I facing that I want to overcome in the next period of time?
- What projects do I want to complete at home, work or school in the next 30 days?
- What relationships need to be fixed, healed, stopped or changed over the next period of time?
- What problems am I facing that need to be solved in the next time period?
- What opportunities are in front of me and how will I decide what to do?

Each family member decides for themselves what exactly they want to be coached on. Once they have set a clear, measurable and meaningful goal it's time for the coaching conversation.

The Coaching Conversation as a part of the Family Ritual Protocol™

Coaching conversations can happen anytime between family members and are a true gift to each other. However, during the regular family ritual meeting; brief and focused coaching conversations that occur one person at a time for 5-10 minutes each, as time permits, are so valuable.

106   Copyright ©2021 Revised Edition. The Family Legacy and Cultural Architects. All rights reserved.

CULTURAL ARCHITECTS

Here are the five simple questions for the coach (leader) to ask…
1. What's Important to you today? (Current goal)
2. What are the challenges and possible solutions?
3. What are you learning?
4. What will you do before our next ritual?
5. How can we help?

Nearly all of the talking that happens in a coaching conversation is done by the person being coached (coachee). The coach only asks the 5 questions while everyone else listens quietly. Very brief advising may be helpful if the coachee is stuck. As a rule, the coach speaks 20% of the time and the coachee speaks 80% of the time.

So much more can be learned about how to be a more effective coach. I enjoy training coaches as much as anything else I get to do. However, keep it simple for best results. Don't overcomplicate things. Don't solve the coachee's problems for them. Help them solve them for themselves. You will be glad you did when you see them grow before your very eyes.

Additional important guidelines for successful coaching conversations
- Be a great listener not an advisor, teller, lecturer etc. Be quick to listen and slow to speak as a coach.
- Don't push your own agenda. Allow the coachee to own their own process, decisions, and actions.
- Be curious and use your limited 20% talk time to ask a few good questions. Explore
- Keep the environment safe. Do not allow criticism, sarcasm, cutting remarks by anyone.
- Keep it simple. Follow the Five coaching questions listed above.
- Make sure there are clear and measurable goals to start with and actions to end with each coaching conversation.
- Stay positive and supportive through the entire coaching conversation.

CULTURAL /\RCHITECTS

FAMILY LEGACY FAMILY RITUAL PROTOCOL

Family Ritual-
Idea Tool™

THE FAMILY
REFORMATION PROJECT

The purpose of this tool is to provide you with some solid ideas to choose from when planning out your regular family ritual meetings. The ideas below are a starting place. The only limits to your options are your own creativity and family preferences. You may also want to consider factors such as the age of participants, nutritional restrictions, time constraints, and physical limitations. If you have additional ideas that you are willing to share with other families, go to the Family Legacy social media pages and post your ideas.

As you plan for your family ritual meetings, periodically review the sections in Chapter 4 entitled:
- Getting the most from your family legacy work and
- Tips for effectively leading your own Family Legacy Protocols

Food Ideas
- *Family Favorites*- Have everyone submit a favorite meal request and put them on the menu.
- *Tour of Nations*- Mexican, Italian, Thai, Chinese, American, Vegetarian- over 200 to choose from.
- *Chef's Choice*- Assign a different Chef for each ritual and empower them to see it all the way through from start to finish. Menu selection, shopping, preparation, clean up. (With help of course)
- *Family Traditions*- List the family traditional favorites passed down from ages past and teach family members how to prepare them at each ritual.
- *Sandwich Shop*- Gather ingredients and let everyone prepare their own sandwich and sides.
- *Pizza Factory*- Gather ingredients and allow everyone to make their own personal pizza with sides.
- *Take Out*- Let's not forget about the ease and convenience of ordering take out or delivery from a favorite family establishment.

Story Ideas
- What is your favorite memory as a child? Teenager? Adult?
- What was the most rewarding part of the last week? (Month, year)
- What was the most challenging part of the last week? (Month, year)
- What is one thing that you are really excited about in your life right now?

CULTURAL /\RCHITECTS

- What is one of your biggest or most important life achievements? Why?
- What do you want your family to know about you more than anything else right now?
- What is one of the things you love about the person to your right?
- What are you grateful for in your life right now?
- What are you looking forward to in your future? Why?
- What is the worst job you've ever had? Why? (Best job?)
- What is a big life dream for you?
- If you could change anything in the world, what would you change and why?
- If you could solve any problem in the world, what would it be and why?
- What is stopping you from doing something you really want to do but haven't done yet?
- What are you best and/or worst memories from your school days?
- What do you like best about our family and why?
- What would you like to change about our family and why?
- Answer this question in 3 minutes or less.. Who am I?
- Share an experience from your life where you felt like a success or a victor.
- Share an experience from your life where you failed and what you learned from that.
- Share an experience from your life where you really needed help from others.
- Share an experience from your life where overcame a difficult challenge.
- What characteristics best define our family? (Give examples)
- What does it take to be a good friend?
- How do you want to be remembered at the end of your life and what will it take to do that?
- What makes a great family?
- What makes a great marriage?
- What makes a great parent?
- What make a great legacy?
- What would make an epic family vacation or family experience?

Coaching Ideas
See the **Ritual Coaching Tool™** for tips, topics and tools in using a coach approach in the family ritual.

Wisdom Ideas
- Read one chapter in Proverbs per family ritual meeting and have open discussion exploring the meaning, real life personal application, and implications of choosing to follow or not follow wisdom in real life examples.
- Invite everyone to submit a wise saying, quote or thought and have each one share one thought per ritual with discussion following.
- Have everyone answer the question, "What piece of wisdom have you experienced in your life recently and how so exactly"?

- Invite every member to share a prayer request and pray together for the requests.
- Select a book, have everyone read a portion/chapter and then discuss for learning.
- Watch an educational, spiritual, or informative video and discuss for learning. (You Tube, DVD, etc.)
- Pick a topic and invite everyone to share their best piece of wisdom in regard to the topic. (Love, relationships, dating, faith, prayer, hearing God, career, etc.)
- Discuss a recent teaching, sermon, or lecture that was particularly meaningful.

Fun Ideas

- Board games- age appropriate and time appropriate. A 3- hour game of the Settlers of Catan may not work at every ritual, but it is a current favorite in our house. Monopoly, Life, there are thousands of games to choose from. Ask Google :)
- Card games- Go Fish, Uno, Black Jack
- Dominoes, Sequence, Connect Four
- Speak Out- this one is hilarious
- Jam time! If you happen to have musicians in the house, this can be a blast!
- Jokes around the bon fire or fire place
- Home-made malts or dessert bar can be a nice add on
- Outdoor games, Yard games such as yard darts, paintball, corn hole, whiffle ball, bocce ball, croquet
- Round robin tournaments in basketball horse, air-hockey, billiards or foosball
- Watch a family appropriate comedy movie together with popcorn
- Go swimming or take a dip in the hot tub
- Go for a hike together
- Service projects- helping a neighbor, helping out at a feeding kitchen or downtown mission
- Take suggestions from all family members for fun ideas and work through the list

CULTURAL ARCHITECTS

FAMILY LEGACY VENTURE PROTOCOL

Family Legacy-
Venture Protocol 4

THE FAMILY
REFORMATION PROJECT

The purpose of the Family Legacy Venture Protocol™ is to intentionally create a fun, memorable, learning adventure (experience) for the whole family to enjoy annually, while anchoring the moments and milestones of family legacy deep into their hearts and DNA for generations to come.

Definition - The Family Legacy Venture Protocol™ is an annual learning adventure (experience) for the whole family to enjoy that is fun, memorable, and intentional. This protocol combines a family vacation with fun, food, stories, learning adventures, book talks, service projects and coaching conversations to effectively live and leave an enduring family legacy. The experiential nature of the protocol equips future generations to continue this rich practice for generations to come.

Why connect a fun trip or family vacation with a family legacy protocol? Because you get a huge return on your investment of time and money when you do. Because it works!

Why does it work?
It is a fun and feel good that *lasts*! The emotional implant that accompanies a fun and feel good experience causes gene expression and lasting change.

It empowers the family to *grow*! Experiential learning causes deep, accelerated, and lasting growth by design.

It is *multi-generational*! The richness of wisdom that is shared and passed on in an environment of honor, respect and love invigorates legacy.

It is *reproducible*! The framework can be easily learned and done for generations yet contains an infinite variety of possibilities.

It is a *multi-sensory* memory that sticks - This protocol includes fun, rest, food, learning, joy, story, imagination, activity, play and love. It contains gratitude, honor, and vulnerability that build trust and good will.

It creates a *deep bond* in the family! One of most important parts of the family legacy is the connectedness and bond that must be present if it is ever going to be passed on.

It is **intentional!** The Venture Protocols work if you work them. Simple to do and simple not to do. The protocols provide a template for creating an amazing family legacy venture.

The Family Legacy Venture Protocol™ **framework** is another simple, intentional, and powerful set of practices with nearly endless possibilities. There are so many combinations of places to see, trips to take, foods to eat, stories to tell, subjects to cover, books to read, activities to enjoy, and questions to ask.

The Family Legacy Venture™ Framework

Pre-Venture Preparation
- Venture selection
- Joint planning
- Naming the venture
- Shared responsibilities
- Logistics
- Paying for the trip
- Schedule
- Build up
- Book discussion
- Guidelines and agreements

Venture Execution
- Experiential module(s)
- Service project
- Mealtime
- Food
- Fun
- Use of story
- Coaching conversations
- Legacy connection

Post Venture Learning
- Debrief

CULTURAL ARCHITECTS

FAMILY LEGACY VENTURE PROTOCOL

THE FAMILY
REFORMATION PROJECT

Family Venture-
Launch Tool

The leader explains that the Launch Gathering is to introduce the family to the Venture concepts and to get everyone's help and input for the first official Family Legacy Venture. In addition, everyone will have Venture responsibilities of some kind including destination selection, menu and food prep, logistics and planning, facilitating the experience module(s), leading the FUN, planning and leading the service project, book selection and discussion, and cleaning up. The Family Venture is not a spectator event, everyone gets to engage.

With a flip chart and a marker, the leader begins to gather everyone's input. The process for planning the various parts of the Venture framework at the launch gathering is the same. The leader writes a word or short phrase from below at the top of the flip chart while members can use a copy of the Tool worksheet and write their responses. The leader facilitates discussion and a selection process that produces the top agreed upon responses from the family which become the components of the first Family Legacy Venture.

Brainstorm and come up with the top ideas for each one below. Make sure everyone is heard.

Where shall we go?

What to do for fun?

When shall we go?

What book shall we read and discuss? (Optional)

Who is invited?

FAMILY LEGACY VENTURE PROTOCOL

Family Venture-
Advance Planning Tool

THE FAMILY
REFORMATION PROJECT

Each year it's important to plan for the next big family adventure by completing the Family Venture Advance Planning Exercise together. It is essentially the same process as the launch meeting without some of the foundational introductory remarks. Family members can make new location and activity suggestions. You can make new menu requests and different story topics. It's time for new fun activities along with new learning adventures. This exercise also adds an element of learning and opportunity for improvement by inviting feedback from the previous Venture.

Get out the flip chart and markers and go through the process again. It may be fun to invite a different family member to lead the exercise. This will engage people in a new way, equipping them with new leadership skills and mentoring them in how to do this with their own families one day.

Family Venture- Advance Planning Tool™
Planning the next Family Legacy Venture

Who will be leading this planning session?

_____

Learning from the last Family Venture
The leader lets everyone know that you are first going to learn from the last Family Venture and then plan for the next one.

The leader writes, "What worked?" at the top of a blank flip chart page and gets feedback from family members on what worked from the last family venture. The leader writes them down. Make it fun.

The leader writes, "What didn't work?" at the top of a blank flip chart page and gets feedback from family members on what didn't work from the last family venture. The leader writes them down. Make it fun.

The leader writes, "What did we learn?" at the top of a blank flip chart page and gets feedback from family members on what was learned from the last family venture. The leader writes them down. Make it fun. Reflect on valuable responses.

CULTURAL /\RCHITECTS

Planning for the Next Family Venture
With a flip chart and a marker, the leader begins to gather everyone's input. The process for planning the various parts of the Venture framework at the launch gathering is the same. The leader writes a word or short phrase from below at the top of the flip chart while members can use a copy of the Tool worksheet and write their responses. The leader facilitates discussion and a selection process that produces the top agreed upon responses from the family which become the components of the first Family Legacy Venture.

Brainstorm and come up with the top ideas for each one below. Make sure everyone is heard.

Where shall we go?

What to do for fun?

When shall we go?

What book shall we read and discuss? (Optional)

Who is invited?

What shall we eat?

What stories shall we prepare for sharing?

What service project will we do? (Optional)

CULTURAL ARCHITECTS

What is the focus of our experience learning module(s)? e.g. dreams, healing, growth, health, nutrition, EQ

How will we make the legacy connection?

What shall we name the Venture we are planning?

What is the budget and each person's contribution?

Assigning Responsibilities:
Everyone helps out. Who is going to do what? Ask for volunteers and appropriately assign people to the roles below. Roles may require more than one person and members may help out in several roles. Age, giftedness, and fit for the roles should also be considered. Copy the roles below onto a flip chart sheet and put name(s) beside each of the roles as the family sees fit.

ROLE	NAME
Logistics and communication	
Travel Arrangements	
Create a meal Menu	
Food Shopping/ Preparation	
Clean Up	
Book Discussion	
Service Project	
Captain FUN	
Facilitating experience modules	
Facilitating coaching conversations	
Budget and Finances	
Story Time	
Legacy Connection	

CULTURAL ARCHITECTS

THE FAMILY
REFORMATION PROJECT

FAMILY LEGACY VENTURE PROTOCOL

Family Venture-
Agenda Tool ™

In order to maximize the focus and intentionality of the Family Legacy Venture, it is helpful to have an agenda or schedule to follow. It is important for the family venture to strike a balance between planning and free flow in order to address the topics that will build a healthy family legacy. If you want to end up at a specific location, you need a map. At the same time, once in a while you can do a little exploring along the way.

Planning out the details make it much more likely that each Venture will be executed effectively for the good of everyone and for the family legacy. I've provided a simple tool to plan and distribute to everyone prior to each family venture so everyone is prepared for their assignments and their contributions. At first, it may seem overwhelming to think about including all of these new practices into a vacation. However, once you are familiar with them it is fairly easy and very much a natural flow of conversation. The difference is that you are doing things intentionally in order to connect and impact the family.

Family Venture Agenda Tool ™

The Purpose of this tool is to help you plan the details of an individual family venture, put it into a schedule, and to share it with family participants. Fill in the specific details for each item below.

Date	Times	Location Specifics

Travel Arrangements and /Details

Cost and Payment Instructions

CULTURAL ARCHITECTS

Packing List
- Clothes
- Instruments
- Computers
- Games
- Other

Food

What is the Food Budget?

What's on the menu?

Who's doing the grocery shopping?

Who's doing the food preparation, cooking and set up?

Who's doing meal clean up (schedule)

	Breakfast	Lunch	Dinner
Day 1			
Day 2			
Day 3			
Day 4			
Day 5			
Day 6			
Day 7			

Story

What story topics should everyone prepare for?

CULTURAL ΛRCHITECTS

Book Discussion

What Book are we reading and when is the discussion scheduled

What Book	When is Discussion Scheduled

Experiential Module Detail

What are we doing?

What are we focused on learning?

Instructions for preparation

Coaching Conversations Detail

FUN

What are the family fun activity details?

Family Legacy Connection Detail

Daily Schedule

Times	Day 1	Day 2	Day 3	Day 4	Day 5

By using this tool, you can both plan intentionally and communicate the plan to family members. You will also have a record of your Ventures to keep so you can see what you've covered and what is left to cover that is important to your family legacy. In addition, you are leaving a wonderful codified record of how you did family that you can pass on to generations to come that will reinforce the practice of the family legacy venture.

Family Venture Service Project (Optional)
Serving others together as a family leaves a powerful and lasting imprint on everyone involved. As you decide whether or not to include a service project in your family venture, consider the following benefits doing so.
- Blesses other people
- Blesses your own family
- Demonstrates empathy and service to others
- Provides a growth experience for members
- Can double as one of your experience modules

CULTURAL ∧RCHITECTS

FAMILY LEGACY VENTURE PROTOCOL

Family Venture- Service Project

The service project can be large or small. It can take up several days or just a few hours. From building a home in Mexico for a poor family to visiting the elderly in a care facility, or from sprucing up the lawn to painting a relative or neighbors home, there are endless possibilities to serve others. You will model social responsibility and a compassion for people to your family with long term, and even eternal impact.

Venture Service Project Tool™

The purpose of this tool is to help you plan the details of a service project as a part of your Family Legacy Venture.

Details of the service project.

Date	Time	Location

What about the project recipients? (Person, family or organization details)

What will we be doing?

Who will be doing what?

CULTURAL ARCHITECTS

How should we prepare ourselves?

Clothes	
Supplies	
Finances	
Emotionally	
Spiritually	
Physically	
Transportation Details	

Describe the why behind this particular project selection…

Specific project instructions (safety, process, guidelines)

Remember, the service project can be formal or informal in nature. Serving an organization works great! Serving one another in the family or a particular person in the family intentionally can work great as well.

FAMILY LEGACY VENTURE PROTOCOL

Family Venture-
Book Discussion (Optional)

THE FAMILY
REFORMATION PROJECT

As I mentioned earlier in this chapter, including a book discussion may or may not be something you choose to add to the Family Legacy Venture. Vocabulary and age appropriateness, along with subject matter and comprehension are all important considerations in making a book selection should you choose to include it.

Here are some compelling reasons to include a book discussion as a part of your family venture:

- Third party expertise allows the family to "discover" ideas together from an expert instead of hearing something again from mom and dad.
- A book is lasting and can be referred to in the future
- Leaders are readers. It's always a good idea to foster reading, comprehension and discussion for growth.
- Modeling a value for learning in your family has long reaching effects.
- Prayerful selection can bring a spiritual growth opportunity as well.
- Discussion creates an opportunity to listen and share with one another for deeper connection.
- Discussion then leads to application of concepts into real life with supportive accountability.
- Book selection can address a family legacy value, practice or characteristic to further equip members to "live it to give it"!

Venture Book Discussion Tool™

The purpose of this tool is to help you select a book and execute an effective discussion as an important part of your Family Legacy Venture.

Book Selection
If you've completed the Launch Gathering Tool™ or the Advanced Planning Tool™ you've likely already got some good ideas for selecting a book. Here are some other things to weigh in your decision.

The following questions are primarily for mom and dad to answer with input from family members.

What topics or areas of growth are relevant to your family in this season of life? e.g. forgiveness, healing, growth in health, nutrition, relationships, business, financial stewardship, effective prayer, dating, marriage, divorce recovery, career selection, etc.

What family legacy characteristics or values do you want to emphasize or grow in as a family? e.g. trust, honor, courage, leadership, hearing God's voice, etc.

Once you have selected a book, purchase enough copies for each person and give 4-8 weeks lead time prior to your venture for everyone to read the book. Tell everyone there will be a discussion and to come to the venture prepared to share your learnings and how you will apply it to your life.

Book Discussion
Make time in your Family Venture schedule for a book discussion with family members. Depending on the size of your family and the value they create from reading the book, I recommend allocating somewhere between 2-3 hours for the entire book discussion.

Provide a relaxed environment free from the noisy distractions of cell phones, television, music, restaurant service etc.

Allow each person to respond to the following questions while everyone practices empathetic listening.

- What was the learning you experienced from reading the book?
- How does it apply specifically to your life?
- How will you put your learning into specific action in your life?

After each person has responded, the leader then asks these two questions to the entire family.

- How specifically does our learning apply to our family as a whole?
- How will we put our learning into specific action as a family moving forward?

Make sure to have someone take notes or even record a video of the discussion in order to capture the insights, learning and commitments to action for the family moving forward.

THE FAMILY
REFORMATION PROJECT

FAMILY LEGACY VENTURE PROTOCOL

Family Venture- Coaching Tool

As you plan for the coaching conversations during the family venture, review the sections in Chapter 4 entitled:
- Getting the most from your family legacy work and
- Tips for effectively leading your own Family Legacy Protocols

Family coaching conversations are one of the distinctive practices that set this entire Family Legacy Model™ apart from any other. The coach approach in the Family Venture protocol brings safety, support, discovery, personal responsibility and practical application together into a five-question conversation that builds families, businesses and communities. During the Venture protocol, a special legacy connection is added to the coaching conversation.

Coaching is one of the most empowering and invigorating modalities in creating growth and success offered today. To bring this into the family ritual and to invest in the personal growth and development of each member is a powerful way to do family. Family coaching is an effective way to build legacy while training our children how to bring coaching into their generations to come.

Venture Coaching Tool

The purpose of this tool is to help you follow a simple coaching conversation with the goal of implanting the legacy lessons and learnings from all of the family venture experiences. Depending on the number of people participating, you may only get to a few members at each mealtime. Be sure to get to everyone over the course of the venture.

Here is the five-question coaching conversation model for use during mealtime in the Family Venture protocol. It is important to bring the context of family legacy into these conversations.

1. What did you experience and observe today? (book, service project, stories, meals, experience modules)

2. What did you learn?

3. How does your learning specifically apply to your life and our family legacy?

4. What will you do specifically moving forward?

5. How can we help?

CULTURAL ARCHITECTS

Additional important guidelines for successful coaching conversations

- Be a great listener not an advisor, teller, lecturer etc. Be quick to listen and slow to speak as a coach.
- Don't push your own agenda. Allow the coachee to own their own process, decisions, and actions.
- Be curious and use your limited 20% talk time to ask a few good questions. Explore.
- Keep the environment safe. Do not allow criticism, sarcasm, cutting remarks by anyone.
- Keep it simple. Follow the Five coaching questions listed above.
- Stay positive and supportive through the entire coaching conversation.

CULTURAL /|RCHITECTS

THE FAMILY
REFORMATION PROJECT

FAMILY LEGACY VENTURE PROTOCOL

Family Venture-Experience Module(s)

By design, the family legacy venture is an experiential module in its own right. However, I agree with the research that suggests including at least one focused learning experience during the course of the venture produces long lasting benefits. Especially when we connect the experience to family identity and legacy!

What do you want to teach your family?
How to dream? How to hear God? How to be successful in marriage, parenting, or on the job? How to heal? How to bring healing to others? How to be good stewards of their health, finances and talents? What about teaching them to be grateful, generous, and loving? What about teaching them how to make good decisions?

There is a nearly endless list of things to teach our families to help them succeed in life and legacy. Choosing to teach them by intentionally giving them an experience is wise. Giving them an experience equips them to give similar experiences to their children and grandchildren.

Do not underestimate the eternal transformative power and results to your family legacy from a simple and intentional experience.

At the most basic level, an experiential learning module has four parts:

- **Set up** - Where a leader talks about the purpose, value and opportunities of the experience along with the detailed instructions of what to do.

- **Execution** - Where members have the experience.

- **Learning** - Where participants share what they learned in the experience, about themselves, their thinking, others, the topic, the world, their faith, etc.

- **Application** - Where participants share how they will apply the learning in specific areas of their lives.

Venture Experience Module Tool

The purpose of this tool is to help you successfully plan and execute an experience learning module as a part of your family legacy venture.

CULTURAL /\RCHITECTS

What do you want to teach your family?

```
[                                                    ]
```

(See suggestions above)

What experience can you create that will accomplish that?
Service project? Book? Visit to Kennedy Space Center or Noah's Ark in Kentucky? Be creative.

```
[                                                    ]
```

Planning the Module - Fill in your thoughts for each of the four parts detailed above for your specific experience.

- Set up- What are you doing? Why? What's the value? What are the instructions?

```
[                                                    ]
```

- Execution- Enjoying the experience together. Make it Fun.

```
[                                                    ]
```

- Learning - Ask the questions. What is the learning from the experience? How does this relate to family legacy?

```
[                                                    ]
```

- Application- Ask the questions. How specifically will you apply the learning moving forward?

```
[                                                    ]
```

CULTURAL ARCHITECTS

THE FAMILY
REFORMATION PROJECT

FAMILY LEGACY VENTURE PROTOCOL

Family Venture-Legacy Tool

Believe it or not, every single aspect of the Family Venture is directly connected to your family legacy. As are all of the Family Legacy Protocols. The choice you make to do family life the way you do is living the legacy that you will leave. Choosing to intentionally give your family emotionally implanted experiences connected to important family values, identity, purpose and practice will impact the trajectory of your family. Your choices will determine your family legacy.

The big idea here is to simply connect the stories, experiences, and coaching conversations you select in your family venture to the heart and essence of your family values, purpose and character. Through intentionality and the skilled use of powerful questions in a time of debrief, you can connect the "doing" and the "learning" to the "being" and the "becoming".

Venture Legacy Tool

The purpose of this tool is to help you be intentional in the use of powerful questions during your family venture to make a strong legacy connection in family members.

It is important to have the legacy connection in mind as you are planning the various parts of the family venture. When selecting and planning the destination, book, service project, story topics, experience modules and so forth, think family legacy values, identity, purpose and practice.

As you are planning ask yourself these questions.

1. How can I reinforce our family true identity?

2. What does our family need in this season to more fully step into our family values, purpose, and mission?

3. What is the best and most practical book out there on healing, trust, honor, courage, leadership or any other family core characteristic?

4. What kind of service project will cause the family to grow in a specific character quality we want to build in our family?

5. What story topics will address and reinforce our family true identity, values and purpose?

Your answers to these questions will connect the parts of the family venture to family legacy in an effective way.

Don't over complicate it here. If integrity is a family value, then share stories on examples from life of integrity. If leadership is an aspect of your family mission, choose a book on leadership for discussion. If your family has been devastated by divorce, then choose an experience around healing and forgiveness or divorce recovery and talk about what you are learning.

Keep it simple.

FAMILY LEGACY
M.I.S.S.I.O.N.PROTOCOL

Family Legacy-
M.I.S.S.I.O.N. Protocol 5

THE FAMILY
REFORMATION PROJECT

The purpose of the Family Legacy M.I.S.S.I.O.N. Protocol™ is to equip and empower your family to stay connected and meaningfully engaged in challenging times of need. The protocols provide you with an intentional and effective way to steward your family with wisdom during a time of great vulnerability when mindsets are fashioned that have both real time and generational consequences.

Whether the "need" is an opportunity or crisis for one or more members of the family, the M.I.S.S.I.O.N. is a **m**omentary, **i**ntentional, **s**pecific, and **s**upportive **i**ntervention as **o**ne in response to a **n**eed.

Definition
The M.I.S.S.I.O.N. an intentional way for family to steward the most challenging times in life together, *as one*.

The M.I.S.S.I.O.N. is a way to wisely navigate the rough waters of family crisis and opportunity. The practices provide a framework for how everyone can show up productively during these seasons of challenge in ways that will minimize the destructive potential of these experiences replacing them with life giving, legacy shaping, heart connecting experiences together as a family.

You may choose to activate a Family Legacy M.I.S.S.I.O.N. in the following kinds of circumstances...

- Death of a loved one whether expected or unexpected.
- Sickness or injury, including mental health, addiction treatment or recovery
- Wedding or divorce
- Home purchase
- Bankruptcy or financial distress
- Major transition - new job, retirement, family move, new school, etc.
- New business
- Empty nest
- New birth or adoption
- Moral failures,
- Criminal behavior
- Change or shift around spiritual beliefs
- Goals or achievements - training and competing in a triathlon, finishing a university degree, weight loss
- Vacations or travel

More…

CULTURAL ARCHITECTS

A Family Legacy M.I.S.S.I.O.N. could also include a family "cause based" M.I.S.S.I.O.N.* e.g. starting a non-profit for pancreatic cancer research or building a school or orphanage as a missionary project in honor or remembrance of a family member.

Value

In times of high stress, deep grief, frantic uncertainty, and rapid change people need the support and structure of a process to navigate through the turbulent waters. Families, businesses and organizations are shaken in these times and having a plan for bringing everyone together with clear roles can keep the ship upright and moving forward.

The Family Legacy M.I.S.S.I.O.N. Protocol™ Framework
- M-Momentary
- I- Intentional
- S- Specific
- S- Supportive
- I- Intervention
- O- as One
- N- in response to Need

It is often during a traumatic family event where we are most vulnerable to soul wounds that bring lasting pain, skewed perspectives, and broken relationships in families. These wounds are perhaps the biggest and most dangerous threats to successfully living a powerful family legacy. Many of the mindsets that we struggle with today originated in our genetic donors in times of crisis generations ago. The same will be true of your children and theirs.

Because of the high emotion in these traumatic family life events, the perceptions that we arrive at through those experiences lock into our DNA and we begin expressing deep genetic and outward responses to these perceptions. A mindset is formed and followed, sometimes for generations, resulting in ongoing consequences of fear, distrust, identity drift, performance-based value and the list goes on and on. These mindsets then begin producing their fruit in the lives of those we love. Stewarding these experiences well and governing our thinking in the very moments when so many lasting mindsets are being developed and implanted is wise.

CULTURAL ARCHITECTS

THE FAMILY
REFORMATION PROJECT

FAMILY LEGACY M.I.S.S.I.O.N.PROTOCOL

M.I.S.S.I.O.N. Blueprint-Preparation and Planning Tool

The first exercise the Family Legacy M.I.S.S.I.O.N. Protocol™ is for the Commander to complete the M.I.S.S.I.O.N. Blueprint Preparation Tool. The Commander may want to invite a few others to help in the completion of the Blueprint, but it is not required.

For those of you who have a faith orientation, I recommend that you start this entire process with prayer surrendering and dedicating this entire process to God.

Blueprint Preparation Tool™

Who is assuming the role of Commander of this Family M.I.S.S.I.O.N.?

What is your contact information?

What is the estimated time of duration for this M.I.S.S.I.O.N.? (30-90 days)
Projected Start Date Is:

Projected End Date Is:

Is permission needed to engage in this M.I.S.S.I.O.N.? e.g. the person(s) in crisis...

Who will secure permission from them? By when?

What is the purpose of this M.I.S.S.I.O.N.?

CULTURAL ARCHITECTS

What is the official code name for this Family M.I.S.S.I.O.N.?

What are the outcomes you see for the successful completion of this M.I.S.S.I.O.N.?

Where are things at right now? Describe what "is" as of right now in this moment...

How will we get there from here?

What is needed for the M.I.S.S.I.O.N.? List the details as you understand it.

Activities

Resources

Money

Prayer

CULTURAL ARCHITECTS

Advice

```

```

Wisdom

```

```

Roles

```

```

Skills

```

```

Labor

```

```

Transportation

```

```

Projects

```

```

Events

```

```

Professional support (Pastor, Therapist, Doctor, Coach, Real Estate, Attorney…)

```

```

CULTURAL ARCHITECTS

Complete brain dump of what is needed for the M.I.S.S.I.O.N.

What further research or insights do we need for this M.I.S.S.I.O.N.?

List the names of the family members you want to invite into the M.I.S.S.I.O.N.?

Determine a location and time for the M.I.S.S.I.O.N. Launch meeting and send invites.

Who has the skills and abilities needed from the above list? Match names to needs.

Name - Need

What are the specific timelines or deadlines that are in play for this M.I.S.S.I.O.N.?

What will be your primary means of communication with members? E.g. Facebook Private Group? Group Email Chain? Free Conference Call line? Other?

What potential obstacles can you see getting in the way of this M.I.S.S.I.O.N.?

CULTURAL ARCHITECTS

What solutions to these obstacles do you see?

What obstacles do you need support in coming up with solutions for?

What are potential ways that people could be hurt or impacted negatively in this crisis?

Who specifically is at risk?

What is important to keep in mind as you plan and execute this M.I.S.S.I.O.N. ?

What are the fears that you have as you approach this M.I.S.S.I.O.N.?

How will you overcome those fears?

Who will you, as the Commander, reach out to for support if you get overwhelmed?

Who is second in command should you not be able to complete the M.I.S.S.I.O.N.?

What will be the frequency of your M.I.S.S.I.O.N. Briefs? e.g. Daily? Weekly? Other?

Every M.I.S.S.I.O.N. will only be as effective as the preparation and planning of the Blueprint. Don't take any shortcuts here.

THE FAMILY
REFORMATION PROJECT

FAMILY LEGACY M.I.S.S.I.O.N.PROTOCOL

M.I.S.S.I.O.N. Launch-
Gathering and Assignments

The second exercise in the Family Legacy M.I.S.S.I.O.N. Protocol™ is for the Commander to oversee a M.I.S.S.I.O.N. Launch Gathering and Assignments. This is where the Commander shares the Blueprint and engages with family members and potential participants to assign members to tasks, roles, functions along with specific actions that each will commit to as a part of this M.I.S.S.I.O.N.

M.I.S.S.I.O.N. Launch Tool™

When and where is the Launch?

Who is invited to the Launch?

What is the official name of this M.I.S.S.I.O.N.?

Make copies of the Blueprint for all participants. (Be sensitive when including potentially hurtful or confidential information from the original Blueprint. e.g. names of those who are at risk for being offended or wounded. Etc.)
Pass out copies to all in attendance.

Officially call the M.I.S.S.I.O.N. Launch to order:

1. Once members are present, The Commander will officially call the M.I.S.S.I.O.N. to order and call it by the official mission name by saying...

"I'm officially declaring the launch of a Family M.I.S.S.I.O.N. code named..."

Mission Name:	
Date:	

2. Prayer. This is another appropriate time for an opening prayer of dedication and surrender to God if appropriate for your family.

3. The Commander states that, "the purpose of the gathering is to gain further clarity and commitments around the M.I.S.S.I.O.N. Blueprint."

4. M.I.S.S.I.O.N. Blueprint walk-thru by Commander.

The M.I.S.S.I.O.N. Commander will ask everyone present to listen carefully without interruption so that you can get everything out before asking for input, which you both want and look forward to. Allowing you to download everything will save time answering many of the questions before they are asked. Assure them that their input is valuable and that you will do your best to make sure everyone gets the answers they are seeking.

The Blueprint walk-thru is simply that, a walk-thru of everything in the blueprint as it stands right now. The Commander will take the time to talk about each question and the current answers. It's important to tell everyone that these may be incomplete and that they will be asking for input along the way.

5. Begin the M.I.S.S.I.O.N. Blueprint walk-thru
You may pause and ask for input at any time that you feel it is needed or is appropriate.
CAUTION: Don't take too many bunny trails or you will confuse people and take too much time to complete the Gathering agenda.

6. Specifically ask for input in these sections of the Blueprint. (Assign a note taker here)

What is needed for the M.I.S.S.I.O.N.? Ask, "Are we missing anything here?"

>

Gaining agreement for the primary means of communication. Ask and decide.

What obstacles are there? "Are we missing any here?"

>

Possible solutions that we are missing here?

>

CULTURAL ARCHITECTS

What else is important to keep in mind during this M.I.S.S.I.O.N.?

7. Assignments- Who's in? And what will each do specifically?
   Who will commit to what specifically and exactly? By when? Match names with tasks, roles etc. Making sure that everyone understands that this is a commitment and timely and thorough completion is expected from all.

Who	What	When

- Be careful not to overload anyone
- Be careful to include everyone who is willing and able in appropriate ways
- Take robust notes on this
- Distribute the assignments once completed to all involved

8. The Commander will address final Important expectations concerning the M.I.S.S.I.O.N.
   - Ask the gathering, "How do we need to show up?" and draw out responses, take notes. e.g. kind, patient, on time, supportive, encouraging, loving, complete commitments in full, etc.

Take notes here if desired:

   - What do you need from me (Commander)?

   - What I need from you (Team members)?

   - What we need from each other

9. The Commander will announce details and expectations around the M.I.S.S.I.O.N. Briefs
   - We will be connecting on a regular basis via

   [   ]

   (e.g. conference line, FB)

   - The M.I.S.S.I.O.N. Briefs will be approximately 30-45 minutes in length write out when you will have these below.

Frequency	This Day	The Dates	The Times

   - The purpose of the Brief: to address any updates, needs, progress, changes, etc.
   - The outcome is to move the M.I.S.S.I.O.N. forward keeping everyone in the loop.
   - Be sure to ask if anyone needs specific support regarding completing commitments

10. The Commander will ask if anything has been left unsaid and if there are any further questions outstanding before dismissing the M.I.S.S.I.O.N. Gathering.

11. Gathering Dismissal-
    The Commander will thank everyone who is joining the M.I.S.S.I.O.N. And dismiss everyone with a word of blessing or prayer.

You may be asking, "why is this so formal?" The answer to that question is that by adding a measure of order and formality to this process, it intrinsically adds a measure of seriousness with a heightened level of clarity around expectations and ultimately, a more effective Family Legacy M.I.S.S.I.O.N.

FAMILY LEGACY M.I.S.S.I.O.N.PROTOCOL

M.I.S.S.I.O.N. Brief-
Regular Briefing Meeting

THE FAMILY
REFORMATION PROJECT

The third exercise in the Family Legacy M.I.S.S.I.O.N. Protocol™ is
the Commander's stewardship of the regular briefing meeting called the M.I.S.S.I.O.N.
Brief. This is the ongoing communication between all M.I.S.S.I.O.N. participants that
keeps everyone on track and in the know. This is also the place where opportunities
arise to support one another, address any balls that have been dropped, add new
tasks, comfort each other in setbacks and celebrate wins. It is the regular opportunity to
learn from the journey, to connect with family members and to be strengthened with
support for what lies ahead.

M.I.S.S.I.O.N. Brief Tool™

When are the M.I.S.S.I.O.N. Briefs scheduled?

Day	Date	Time

What is the estimated length of time for the Briefs? (30-45 minutes standard)

What is the means of communication? (conference call, in app, in person, etc.)

Who is invited to the Brief?

CULTURAL ARCHITECTS

Who is the note taker for the Brief?

[   ]

The Basic agenda to follow for each M.I.S.S.I.O.N. Brief is:

1. M.I.S.S.I.O.N. Brief Open
   - Commander officially opens the Brief (prayer optional)
   - Roll Call-   Commander- who's in the Brief

2. M.I.S.S.I.O.N. report from each member (Commander facilitates)
   - What is the status of your individual commitment since our last Brief?

[   ]

   - What worked?

[   ]

   - What didn't?

[   ]

   - What next? Commitment of specific individual action before the next Brief
     Support needed?

[   ]

   - What help or support is needed by member?

[   ]

   - Focused input from other M.I.S.S.I.O.N. members on each report

- Expression of gratitude and thanks specifically by name by Commander

2. M.I.S.S.I.O.N. Learnings and Lessons- (open discussion- Commander lead)
   - What did we learn about ourselves and our family in this M.I.S.S.I.O.N.?

   _____

   - How do these lessons apply to the family moving forward?

   _____

3. M.I.S.S.I.O.N. Affirmations and acknowledgments
   - Commander opens the floor for members to affirm and acknowledge one another
4. M.I.S.S.I.O.N. Celebration
   - The Feast! No celebration is complete without some great FOOD.
   - The Fun! Play game, go for a swim or anything your family considers to be fun.
   - Share the love. No matter the outcome, you came together as one.

It is important for the generations to come to have a written record of the Family M.I.S.S.I.O.N.. Can you imagine what it would have been like for your parents or grandparents to have gone through this and passed down a written record of this journey? What a meaningful sharing of life experience, wisdom, love and learning. By keeping a written and digital copy of your Family M.I.S.S.I.O.N.S, you will equip generations to come with a value and model for doing family together as one in times of crisis.

By following this simple structure, family members will have clarity, accountability and connectedness. Importantly, this simple structure can also be taught to our children and become a better way to do family for generations.

CULTURAL /\RCHITECTS

FAMILY LEGACY M.I.S.S.I.O.N.PROTOCOL

THE FAMILY
REFORMATION PROJECT

M.I.S.S.I.O.N
-Wrap Up and Debrief

The final exercise in The Family Legacy M.I.S.S.I.O.N. Protocol™ is the Commander's stewarding of the final outcomes and debrief along with the lessons learned, the growth experienced and the expression of gratitude and recognition of lasting learnings in what I call the M.I.S.S.I.O.N. Wrap Up and Debrief.

Every M.I.S.S.I.O.N. is momentary and has a clear start and end date. For the crisis that may not be resolved at the time of the pre-planned end date, two things can happen. First, the mission can be extended as is for up to 90 days, with or without a brief respite of 7-14 days. Second, a new M.I.S.S.I.O.N. can be launched with the appropriate modifications that reflect the current status and needs of the crisis and participating members. Launching a new M.I.S.S.I.O.N. would mean repeating the exercises in the protocol.

The wrap up and debrief is an important exercise for the purpose of deeply implanting the lessons and takeaways from the experience into the hearts and DNA of every participant. By focusing on the outcomes, lessons and learnings of the M.I.S.S.I.O.N. in an authentic and vulnerable way, the family is drawn together in gratitude, respect and sense of identity. It is the emotional implantation of the experience that remains "sticky" in the lives of members, especially in the children.

M.I.S.S.I.O.N Wrap Up and Debrief Tool™

Appoint a note taker to capture this for posterity.

1. M.I.S.S.I.O.N. final report out by the Commander
   - What were the specific results of the M.I.S.S.I.O.N.?

   - What were the highlights for you as the Commander?

3. M.I.S.S.I.O.N. Learnings and Lessons (open discussion- Commander lead)
   - What are we learning about ourselves and our family in this M.I.S.S.I.O.N.?

   - How do these lessons apply to the family moving forward?

4. M.I.S.S.I.O.N. Affirmations and acknowledgments
   - Commander opens the floor for members to affirm and acknowledge one another

5. M.I.S.S.I.O.N. Brief Dismissal
   - Commander officially closes the Brief. (Prayer optional)

Depending on your family and the level of detail you prefer, a private Facebook Group or other platform like it may be a helpful way to stay connected to each other in between M.I.S.S.I.O.N. Briefs. This platform can serve you for the follow things…
   - Posting weekly commitments and progress to keep everyone informed
   - Encourage one another
   - Celebrate, honor and support the commitments of your family members
   - Have a little fun together
   - Providing inspiration to each other
   - M.I.S.S.I.O.N. Updates
   - Communicating changing circumstances
   - Reaching out for additional support

The M.I.S.S.I.O.N. Brief, if done well, will be the rudder of the M.I.S.S.I.O.N. ship. It will be a regular instrument reading and course correction for where things are at, what's next, what are we learning and how are we are doing.

FAMILY LEGACY IMPARTATION

Family Legacy-Impartation Protocol 6

THE FAMILY
REFORMATION PROJECT

The purpose of the Family Legacy Impartation Protocol™ is to provide an end of life intentional process for creating an enduring legacy by passing on the most important things in life to our children and grandchildren while teaching them how to do the same. It is a mechanism for passing on the legacy so that it continues to be passed on.

What are the most important things in life to be passed on to our families?

Beyond all of the loving memories, experiences and lessons learned with family, at the end of life, what really matters? After much thought, I believe the answer to this question is

- the *wisdom* of a life lived
- the *blessing* of a father and mother
- the *heavenly blessing* and
- the *stuff* that can't go with us

In order to finish well, it is also important for us to reconcile any

- *unfinished business* with God, people, and the responsibilities we have been stewarding.
- And finally, to *deliver* the Family Legacy Covenant to the next generation.

In my experience, most families do a poor job in nearly all of these areas. High net worth families tend to more thoroughly address passing on the "stuff" because they have a lot and desire to steward it well. In addition, more resources and attention are given to the material aspects of a family legacy in our culture. There's a long line of lawyers, financial planners, investment portfolio managers, business partners and philanthropic enterprises who all have a personal interest in supporting families in making decisions with their "stuff."

But where is our focus when it comes to living life in a way that passes on family identity, core values, mission and character? Where is the urgency to ensure that our families have experienced and understand "how to do family" effectively by instilling simple, intentional core protocols and practices that impart the family wisdom, blessing, and stuff thoughtfully?

The time for action is now.

CULTURAL /|RCHITECTS

Definition

The Family Legacy Impartation Protocol™ is a thoughtful, intentional, and systematic process for meaningfully imparting the most important aspects of life and legacy to our children and grandchildren. It is the "how to" pass on a legacy in an end of life context. Through a set of exercises, tools, worksheets, and check lists you will be equipped to compile a written and video "Legacy Cache" for your family. By preparing this now, you ensure that your legacy will endure in the event of an accidental or early death. Should you be graced with a long life, you will also be prepared for a powerful impartation by sharing this Legacy Cache face to face with your family. Having addressed this protocol will also empower you to make the most of the story times in the other 5 Legacy Protocols.

The Family Legacy Impartation Protocol™ **framework** prioritizes life's most important aspects and provides a pathway to see them implanted deep into the hearts and DNA of the next generation.

Intentionally imparting...
- The Wisdom
- The Blessing
- The Stuff
- The Unfinished Business
- The Family Legacy Generational Covenant

The Wisdom

Intentionally passing on your life's lessons, insights, and revelations on a myriad of topics so that your children and family line can receive the benefits from them and in turn, give them away to benefit others is an amazing gift. Doing this by using the protocols and tools makes it easy as you compile a written and video cache for posterity. We walk you through step by step.

The Blessing

Patterned after the Biblical concept of "blessing", this protocol is dad and or mom's last and best "truth bomb" spoken in love for the good of the children. It is the last loving observations, affirmations, advice, pronouncements, assessments, consequences, hopes and governing activities of the head of the family.

This protocol is the parents last and best expression from the reservoir of their entire life experience with specific children for their greatest good in fulfilling their life purpose. We focus on two primary aspects of the Biblical practice of blessing. First, the loving truth telling from parents to each child. The Biblical idea of blessing may include the good, the bad, the ugly, and the consequence of life choices. It may also include approval, reward, and guidance for the future. Second, the declaration of God's blessing on an individual child He has identified to best steward His own purpose and design in each specific family line.

The Stuff

This Protocol is NOT a detailed road map for the traditional passing on of financial wealth, property and assets. Frankly, material wealth transfer without a coinciding transfer of wisdom, character, values and purpose is simply not enough to shape culture well or leave an enduring and eternal family legacy to the glory of God. We must thoughtfully transfer *both* to our generations.

The Unfinished Business

Actually, this section may be better entitled, "The Finished Business." It is important that we impart "finished business" to our children and not "unfinished business." It is much sweeter to impart the order, clarity, ease and purpose of finished business than to impart the bitter chaos, uncertainty, hardship and aimlessness of unfinished business to those we love.

The Family Legacy Generational Covenant

In order to ensure that that the purposes of God in our family line AND our family legacy are imparted to generation after generation, we have designed an intentional process to officially charge the next generation with this sacred honor. In so doing, the stewardship of continuing the family legacy protocols is placed squarely on the shoulders of the next generation.

The impartation protocol done well will ensure a profound and lasting family legacy for generations to come. As our generations are shown how to build families, businesses and communities, they will also have what they need to shape culture after God's design from the inside out.

FAMILY LEGACY IMPARTATION PROTOCOL

Family Legacy-
Wisdom Treasure Hunt Tool™

THE FAMILY
REFORMATION PROJECT

King Solomon told anyone listening to seek wisdom like you were seeking hidden treasure. There is hidden treasure in the life experiences and lessons learned inside of your parents and grandparents. Inside of others who have gone before you lie the treasures of wisdom waiting for you to discover and receive by doing three amazingly simple yet profound things.

1. Ask a good question
2. Listen to understand the answer
3. Put it into action in your own life

Ask a good question:

- What is your life purpose?
- How did you discover your "life purpose"?
- What are your "core values"? The 6-10 most important values in your life and why?
- What lessons did you learn about forgiveness?
- What lessons did you learn about stress?
- What have you learned from your experiences?
- What are the most impactful experiences you have had in your life and why?
- What are some of the oldest and most interesting stories you remember about family generations back?
- What are some of the biggest mistakes that you made in your life?
- What did you learn from them?
- What are some of the most difficult challenges you had in your life?
- What did you do?
- What did you learn from them?
- What is the life wisdom in these experiences?
- What would you do differently in your life if you could?
- What regrets do you have in life and why?
- What are some of your biggest achievements or successes?
- What did it take to make those happen?
- What did those experiences teach you?

CULTURAL ARCHITECTS

What are some of the most important things you've learned about?

- Relationships
- Parenting
- Trust
- Work and career
- Marriage
- Divorce
- Family
- Friendship
- Business

What are some of the most valuable lessons you have learned about money and finances?

- What is the life wisdom you've gathered in regard to building a healthy family?
- What is the life wisdom you've gathered in regard to religion and faith?
- What is the life wisdom you've gathered in regard to government and politics?
- What is the life wisdom you've gathered in regard to education and learning?
- What is the life wisdom you've gathered in regard to business and work?
- What is the life wisdom you've gathered in regard to entertainment and fun?
- What is the life wisdom you've gathered in regard to the media?

Choose to deeply *listen* for the purpose of understanding. Gather the answers and the wisdom like you would gather the jewels and gold bars into a treasure chest to keep them. I recommend that you record in writing and or by video so that you can keep the treasures of wisdom that you have found. Journal the learning during or after a powerful conversation. Pull out your smart phone and record your conversations.

Choose to *put wisdom into practice* by applying them in your own life day by day. Ask for God's help. Just do it! When it's time to make a decision, review your treasure chest full of insight, intelligence, understanding and wisdom and then follow the advice in making your decision.

CULTURAL ＡRCHITECTS

THE FAMILY
REFORMATION PROJECT

FAMILY LEGACY IMPARTATION PROTOCOL

Family Legacy-
Wisdom Impartation Protocol Tool™

Choose to be prepared to share the wisdom you have to give when the time is right by thoughtfully completing the following exercise. Whether you share your wisdom one on one while fishing, with the whole family gathered around you in a Family Legacy Encounter, or at an end of life family gathering by compiling your life wisdom in writing and or by video, you will be ready and ensure that your family benefits from your life lived.

Imparting the Wisdom
What are the most important pieces of wisdom you want to pass on to your children and the generations that follow? After each of the topics below, thoughtfully, prayerfully, share from the treasures of wisdom that are stored inside of you.

Potential topics based on areas that King Solomon addressed in the book of Proverbs.

- Love

- Marriage

- Family

- Parenting

- Business

CULTURAL ARCHITECTS

- Sexuality

- Relationships

- Leadership

- Being a good neighbor

- Conflict resolution

- Being a good listener

- Work habits

- Financial stewardship

CULTURAL ARCHITECTS

- Self-control

- Physical health

- Emotional health

- Spiritual health

- Life and death

- Power of words

- Building communities

- Good and bad character

CULTURAL ARCHITECTS

- Perils of foolishness

  [ ]

- Warnings of alcoholism

  [ ]

- Consequences of sexual perversion

  [ ]

- Legacy planning

  [ ]

- Friendship

  [ ]

- Wealth creation

  [ ]

- Wealth transfer

  [ ]

- Poverty

  [ ]

- Prosperity

- Social justice

- Longevity

- Sustainability

- Healing

- More

I strongly encourage you to make both a written and video record of all of the impartation protocols. By writing them out first, you can more completely and easily share them on video. This is also important to do so that in case of an unexpected death, there is a recorded legacy in place for your family.

THE FAMILY
REFORMATION PROJECT

FAMILY LEGACY IMPARTATION PROTOCOL

Family Legacy- Crafting the Parental Blessing Tool™

The purpose of this tool is to help you craft specific *parental* blessings for your children and grandchildren patterned after how these blessings appear in the scriptures.

Instructions:
- Keep it simple
- Follow the six-step process below
- Write them down and/or record them on video
- Deliver them in person, face to face if at all possible

Step One: Put yourself in a calm, comfortable state and say a prayer requesting God's help in this process. Give yourself uninterrupted time and space.

Step Two: Reread Genesis Chapter 49 where Jacob blesses his twelve sons.

Step Three: Review the guidelines and substance sections in chapter 10 above and take them into account as you prepare the parental blessings.

Step Four: Craft the individual parental blessings for each child or grandchild by mindfully determining from your heart, *the most important truths for your generations to hear from you that will have the greatest likelihood of supporting them in fulfilling their life purpose and mission.*

Write down the names of each of you children and then after each name, work through the bullet list below and write down notes of the things that come to mind for them. You may or may not have something written for each person and each bullet point. This serves as a guide for you to follow in crafting the parental blessings.

The **substance** of *parental* blessings in scripture are reflected in the Impartation Protocols™ and include:

- Identity statements
- Acknowledgements of character strengths
- Acknowledgements of character flaws
- Affirmations
- Life purpose declarations
- Business advice
- Truth-telling in love
- Curses and punishment

CULTURAL ARCHITECTS

- Leadership roles within the family
- Assignment of responsibilities
- Cultural Engagement
- Foretelling of upcoming battles and winning strategy advice

Names of children and/or grandchildren and your notes for each one below.

NAME	NOTES

CULTURAL ARCHITECTS

Step Five: Write down each name again and then craft a complete parental blessing statement from the notes you've made above.

NAME	CRAFTED PARENTAL BLESSING

Six: Deliver the blessings by either reading them while recording yourself on video or in a face to face gathering of family. The video recording is to ensure that you impart the parental blessing even if there would be an unexpected death. If you find yourself in a known end of life scenario, you may want to deliver the blessings face to face.

Remember, our Family Legacy Coaches are here to assist you at any point along the way as you implement the protocols. Don't hesitate to reach out for support.

CULTURAL ᐱRCHITECTS

FAMILY LEGACY IMPARTATION PROTOCOL

Family Legacy-
Crafting the Heavenly Blessing Tool™

THE FAMILY
REFORMATION PROJECT

The purpose of this tool is to help you craft a specific *heavenly* blessing for the child you have identified as God's choice in stewarding His purposes for your family line patterned after how this blessing appears in scripture.

Instructions:
- Keep it simple
- Follow the six-step process below
- Write your work down and/or record them on video
- Deliver the *heavenly* blessing in person, face to face if at all possible

One: Put yourself in a calm, comfortable state and say a prayer requesting God's help in this process. Give yourself uninterrupted time and space.

Two: Reread Genesis Chapter 49:22-26, where Jacob blesses Joseph.

Three: Review the *heavenly* blessing substance section in chapter 10 and take them into account as you prepare the *heavenly* blessing.

Four: Craft the individual *heavenly* blessing for the child by mindfully determining from your heart, in consultation with God, *the most important things God has for them to empower them as they faithfully steward God's purposes in the family line.*

Write down the name of the one identified and then work through the bullet list below and write down notes of the things that come to mind. You may or may not have something written for each bullet point. This serves as a guide for you to follow in crafting the heavenly blessings.

Jacob's *heavenly* blessing to Joseph in Gen. 49:22-26, was distinct in substance from the parental blessings to his brothers and included:

- Identity statements
- Acknowledgement of Joseph's good stewardship and fruitfulness to God's purposes for the family line historically.
- Prophetic declaration of Josephs fruitfulness in the future
- Historical accounts of Joseph's battles and victories
- Recognition that God's hand was upon Joseph
- Recognition that God actively shepherded Joseph
- Acknowledgement that God's choice in Joseph was rock solid

CULTURAL /\RCHITECTS

- Acknowledgement that Jacob's God also helped Joseph
- Declaration that God's blessing was on Joseph
- Declaration that all of Jacob's blessings rested on Joseph
- Recognition of Joseph's responsibilities as the "prince among his brothers"
- He included a multi-generational *heavenly blessing* to Joseph's sons Ephraim and Manasseh Gen. 48, making it clear who the purposes of God for the family line would be stewarded by.

NAME	NOTES

Five: Craft a complete heavenly blessing from your notes above.

Name   the *heavenly* blessing

NAME	The *HEAVENLY* BLESSING

Six: Deliver the heavenly blessing by either reading it while recording yourself on video or in a face to face gathering of family. The video recording is to ensure that you impart the *heavenly* blessing even if there would be an unexpected death. If you find yourself in a known end of life scenario, you may want to deliver the blessing face to face.

Remember, our Family Legacy Coaches are here to assist you at any point along the way as you implement the protocols. Don't hesitate to reach out for support.

CULTURAL /\RCHITECTS

THE FAMILY
REFORMATION PROJECT

FAMILY LEGACY IMPARTATION PROTOCOL

Family Legacy-
Imparting the Stuff Form No. 1
Specific Gift of Personal Items

Passing on specific gifts to those who have a special place in your heart can be meaningful. Valuable items like jewelry, family Bibles, pieces of artwork, antiques, as well as, things that have special meaning and sentiment rather than a significant monetary value should be intentionally passed on with purpose. Including the emotional why or purpose for giving the specific items to specific people, along with any relevant insights on how to steward it well, is important to ensuring a powerful family legacy. When you complete this form, date and initial the bottom right of each page and place a copy with your Will. If you would like to give more items than are included in this form, copy and fill out as many pages as you need to make all of your gifts and put copies of all of them with your Will.

Upon my death, I [_____] (name of person making gift)
want the following:
- These specific possessions given to designated people or organizations upon my death
- The location of the item
- The emotional why, story, and purpose for giving it to this recipient
- The relevant insights on how to steward it well and connection to family legacy

Gift One:
To:
Description of the Item

[_____]

Location of the item

[_____]

The emotional why, story and purpose for giving to this recipient

[_____]

The relevant insights on how to steward it well and connection to family legacy

[_____]

CULTURAL ARCHITECTS

Gift Two:
To:
Description of the Item

[   ]

Location of the item

[   ]

The emotional why, story and purpose for giving to this recipient

[   ]

The relevant insights on how to steward it well and connection to family legacy

[   ]

Gift Three:
To:
Description of the Item

[   ]

Location of the item

[   ]

The emotional why, story and purpose for giving to this recipient

[   ]

The relevant insights on how to steward it well and connection to family legacy

[   ]

Gift Four:
To:
Description of the Item

[   ]

Location of the item

[   ]

CULTURAL ARCHITECTS

The emotional why, story and purpose for giving to this recipient

The relevant insights on how to steward it well and connection to family legacy

Gift Five:
To:
Description of the Item

Location of the item

The emotional why, story and purpose for giving to this recipient

The relevant insights on how to steward it well and connection to family legacy

Gift Six:
To:
Description of the Item

Location of the item

The emotional why, story and purpose for giving to this recipient

The relevant insights on how to steward it well and connection to family legacy

CULTURAL ARCHITECTS

Gift Seven:
To:
Description of the Item

Location of the item

The emotional why, story and purpose for giving to this recipient

The relevant insights on how to steward it well and connection to family legacy

Gift Eight:
To:
Description of the Item

Location of the item

The emotional why, story and purpose for giving to this recipient

The relevant insights on how to steward it well and connection to family legacy

CULTURAL ARCHITECTS

THE FAMILY
REFORMATION PROJECT

FAMILY LEGACY IMPARTATION PROTOCOL

Family Legacy-
Imparting the Stuff Form No. 2
Vital Personal Information

Emergency Contacts:

Primary Personal Contact(s): Please contact them in the event of an emergency:

1. Name:

Phone Number:

E-Mail Address:

2. Name:

Phone Number:

E-Mail Address:

3. Name:

Phone Number:

E-Mail Address:
:

Primary Work Contact(s):

1. Name:

Phone Number:

E-Mail Address:

2. Name:

Phone Number:

E-Mail Address:

3. Name: _____

   Phone Number: _____

   E-Mail Address: _____

Name and Phone Number of Person Authorized to Make Health Care Decisions:

   Name: _____

   Phone Number: _____

   E-Mail Address: _____

Location of Living Will, Health Care Power of Attorney, Will, Power of Attorney and other Estate Documents:

_____

Location of Passport, Birth Certificate, Car and House Titles & Keys:

_____

Location of Safety Deposit Box & Key: _____

Location of Unpaid Bills: _____

Location of Checkbooks: _____

My Social Security Number is: _____

List of Doctors:

Name _____ Type _____

Phone Number _____

CULTURAL ARCHITECTS

Name [   ] Type [   ]

Phone Number [   ]

Name [   ] Type [   ]

Phone Number [   ]

Name [   ] Type [   ]

Phone Number [   ]

Name, Phone Number, and E-mail of Attorney:

[   ]

Name, Phone Number, and E-mail of Accountant:

[   ]

Name and Phone Number of Church and Other Organizations to Which I Belong:

[   ]

Location of any storage facility, access code, and location of a key:

[   ]

Miscellaneous Additional Personal Information

[   ]

CULTURAL ARCHITECTS

THE FAMILY
REFORMATION PROJECT

FAMILY LEGACY IMPARTATION PROTOCOL

Family Legacy-
Imparting the Stuff Form No. 3
List of All Bank Accounts

Name of Bank or Credit Union:

Account Number:

Any Access Code/Password:

Web address for online Banking:

Account Balance and Date of Balance:

Name of Bank or Credit Union:

Account Number:

Any Access Code/Password:

Web address for online Banking:

Account Balance and Date of Balance:

Name of Bank or Credit Union:

Account Number:

Any Access Code/Password:

Web address for online Banking:

Account Balance and Date of Balance:

CULTURAL ARCHITECTS

Name of Bank or Credit Union:

Account Number:

Any Access Code/Password:

Web address for online Banking:

Account Balance and Date of Balance:

Name of Bank or Credit Union:

Account Number:

Any Access Code/Password:

Web address for online Banking:

Account Balance and Date of Balance:

Location of checkbook, checks and statements:

CULTURAL ARCHITECTS

FAMILY LEGACY IMPARTATION PROTOCOL

The Family Legacy-
Imparting the Stuff Form No.4
List of All Investments and Non-Bank Accounts

THE FAMILY
REFORMATION PROJECT

Investment Accounts:

Name of Investment Company:

Name of Contact Person at Company (if any:

Company Phone No. and/or E-Mail Address:

Account Number:

Account Access Code/Password (if any:

Name of Investment Company:

Name of Contact Person at Company (if any:

Company Phone No. and/or E-Mail Address:

Account Number:

Account Access Code/Password (if any):

Name of Investment Company:

Name of Contact Person at Company (if any):

Company Phone No. and/or E-Mail Address:

Account Number:

Account Access Code/Password (if any):

CULTURAL ARCHITECTS

Name of Investment Company:

Name of Contact Person at Company (if any:

Company Phone No. and/or E-Mail Address:

Account Number:

Account Access Code/Password (if any:

Name of Investment Company:

Name of Contact Person at Company (if any:

Company Phone No. and/or E-Mail Address:

Account Number:

Account Access Code/Password (if any:

Name of Investment Company:

Name of Contact Person at Company (if any:

Company Phone No. and/or E-Mail Address:

Account Number:

Account Access Code/Password (if any):

Name of Investment Company:

Name of Contact Person at Company (if any):

Company Phone No. and/or E-Mail Address:

Account Number:

Account Access Code/Password (if any):

CULTURAL ARCHITECTS

THE FAMILY
REFORMATION PROJECT

FAMILY LEGACY IMPARTATION PROTOCOL

The Family Legacy-
Imparting the Stuff Form No.5
List of Non-Liquid Assets

If you have pieces of furniture, art work, books, stamp collections, jewelry, cars, properties, or other items that are particularly valuable they should be included in a written list, so it is clear what is to be done with them at end of life.

Real Estate:

Address of Real Estate:

Percentage Ownership Interest:

Type (House, Condo, Time Share, etc.):

Outstanding Loan Balance & Date of Balance:

Address of Real Estate:

Percentage Ownership Interest:

Type (House, Condo, Time Share, etc.):

Outstanding Loan Balance & Date of Balance:

Address of Real Estate:

Percentage Ownership Interest:

Type (House, Condo, Time Share, etc.):

Outstanding Loan Balance & Date of Balance:

Vehicles: Autos, Trucks, Boats, Motorcycles, RV's, etc.:

Year, Type & Description of Vehicle:

Outstanding Loan Balance & Date of Balance:

CULTURAL ARCHITECTS

Year, Type & Description of Vehicle:

Outstanding Loan Balance & Date of Balance:

Year, Type & Description of Vehicle:

Outstanding Loan Balance & Date of Balance:

Year, Type & Description of Vehicle:

Outstanding Loan Balance & Date of Balance:

Year, Type & Description of Vehicle:

Outstanding Loan Balance & Date of Balance:

Disability Policies:

Name of Company:

Contact Information:

Name of Company:

Contact Information:

Collectibles:

Gold or Other Metals, Coins, Jewelry, Loose Gem Stones, Art Work, Fire Arms, etc.:

Description & Where They Are Located:

Approximate Value (If known):

Description & Where They Are Located:

Approximate Value (If known):

Description & Where They Are Located:

Approximate Value (If known):

Description & Where They Are Located:

Approximate Value (If known):

Miscellaneous Non-Liquid Assets:
Including Limited Partnership Interests:
Description of Assets(s) & Where They Are Located:

CULTURAL ARCHITECTS

Description of Assets(s) & Where They Are Located:

Description of Assets(s) & Where They Are Located:

Description of Assets(s) & Where They Are Located:

Description of Assets(s) & Where They Are Located:

Description of Assets(s) & Where They Are Located:

FAMILY LEGACY IMPARTATION PROTOCOL

Family Legacy-
Unfinished Business Form No. 1

FUNERAL, BURIAL, CREMATION, MEMORIAL SERVICE INSTRUCTIONS

OR

☐   I would like a more non-traditional memorial service (for example: a memorial service with lots of food, drink, story-telling, and fun). Please list your preferences for your memorial service as follows:

```
[                                                                        ]
[                                                                        ]
[                                                                        ]
[                                                                        ]
[                                                                        ]
[                                                                        ]
```

The following are my preferences in the various matters related to my final arrangements (fill out all that apply):

Name of florist to use: [   ]

I would prefer the following types of flowers:

```
[                                                                        ]
[                                                                        ]
```

In lieu of flowers, please send a donation to:

```
[                                                                        ]
```

List of Music to Be Played:

```
[                                                                        ]
[                                                                        ]
```


CULTURAL ARCHITECTS

Any funeral/burial arrangements should be made through:
(Name funeral home or another provider).

☐ I have / ☐ I have not attached a list of all the people to be contacted upon my death. (if attaching a list of people to be contacted please include both names and phone numbers)

☐ I have / ☐ I have not attached a photo to be used with my obituary, program, and all other related purposes.

Additional Instructions:

CULTURAL ARCHITECTS

Please use the following for my obituary (Complete if you want to write your own obituary):

[ ] I would prefer not to specify the details in connection with my death and do notwant an obituary published. Instead,

[ ] I would like for _____

to make all decisions in connection with the final arrangements upon my death.

_____
Signature

_____
Printed Name

_____
Date of Signature

CULTURAL /\RCHITECTS

FAMILY LEGACY IMPARTATION PROTOCOL

Family Legacy-
Unfinished Business Form No. 2

THE FAMILY
REFORMATION PROJECT

LISTS OF PEOPLE AND ORGANIZATIONS TO BE NOTIFIED UPON YOUR DEATH

No matter how close we are with our spouse, partner, friends or family members, it is unlikely that they will know all of the people that should be told of your death and how to get in touch with each of them. This includes friends, work associates, neighbors, etc. Provide the name of each person and the most appropriate way to contact them.

Name of Person:	Contact Information:

CULTURAL ARCHITECTS

Family Legacy Unfinished Business Form No. 2
ORGANIZATIONS TO BE NOTIFIED UPON DEATH AND ACTIONS TO BE TAKEN

Many organizations we belong to (churches, health clubs, country clubs, civic, etc. or services we subscribe to (lawn services, insect control, credit reporting alerts, Angie's list, etc. must be notified of our deaths to not only cancel memberships and services but to stop automatic renewals if they have a credit card or bank draft on file. Even if the cards are cancelled and bank accounts are frozen after death, if the services aren't actually cancelled, they may be able to make a claim against your estate. In addition, in the case of memberships in clubs, there may be a locker that needs to be cleaned out or similar requirements. Please list all organizations that should be notified of your death and how to contact them as well as provide the information needed for others to cancel any memberships, service accounts, etc. as well as list any additional action that may be required like cleaning out lockers.

Name of Organization: _____
Contact Information: _____
Membership No. or Service Agreement No.: _____
Password, User Name or Other Data Needed to Cancel: _____
Further Action to be Taken and Information Needed to Take Action: _____
_____

Name of Organization: _____
Contact Information: _____
Membership No. or Service Agreement No.: _____
Password, User Name or Other Data Needed to Cancel: _____
Further Action to be Taken and Information Needed to Take Action: _____
_____

Name of Organization: _____
Contact Information: _____
Membership No. or Service Agreement No.: _____
Password, User Name or Other Data Needed to Cancel: _____
Further Action to be Taken and Information Needed to Take Action: _____
_____

Name of Organization: _____
Contact Information: _____
Membership No. or Service Agreement No.: _____
Password, User Name or Other Data Needed to Cancel: _____
Further Action to be Taken and Information Needed to Take Action: _____
_____

CULTURAL ARCHITECTS

THE FAMILY
REFORMATION PROJECT

FAMILY LEGACY IMPARTATION PROTOCOL

Family Legacy- Unfinished Business Form No. 3

PERSONAL DIGITAL FOOTPRINT INFORMATION

COMPUTER, EMAIL, CELLPHONE, ACCOUNTS AND OTHER PASSWORDS

Home 1:
Address: _____
Security Code: _____
Garage Keypad Code: _____
Location of Keys: _____

Home 2:
Address: _____
Security Code: _____
Garage Keypad Code: _____
Location of Keys: _____

Phone Numbers and Passwords:
Phone number: _____
Username/Password_____

Phone number: _____
Username/Password_____

Phone number: _____
Username/Password_____

Email Addresses and Passwords:
Email Address: _____
Username/Password_____

Email Address: _____
Username/Password_____

Email Address: _____
Username/Password_____

Email Address: _____
Username/Password_____

CULTURAL ARCHITECTS

Home Wi Fi Network
Name of home wi-fi network: _____
Username / Password _____

Computer Passwords:
Description and location of computer(s
Computer: _____
Username/Password: _____

Description and location of computer(s
Computer: _____
Username/Password: _____

Description and location of computer(s
Computer: _____
Username/Password: _____

Description and location of computer(s
Computer: _____
Username/Password: _____

On-line Apps and Accounts:
(Amazon, eBay, Facebook, Instagram, Expedia, Delta, etc.

Web Address: _____
Username/Password: _____

Web Address: _____
Username/Password: _____

Web Address: _____
Username/Password: _____

Web Address: _____
Username/Password: _____

Web Address: _____
Username/Password: _____

Web Address: _____
Username/Password: _____

CULTURAL ARCHITECTS

List all other passwords and access codes: (storage, gate access, padlocks, briefcases)

CULTURAL ARCHITECTS

FAMILY LEGACY IMPARTATION PROTOCOL

Family Legacy Unfinished Business Form No. 4

THE FAMILY
REFORMATION PROJECT

LIST OF ALL LOANS AND MORTGAGES

For accurate Financial Planning purposes, please provide account balances and the date of the balance where indicated below.

Mortgages and Home Equity Loans:

Name of Lender: _____
Address of Real Estate: _____
Loan Number: _____
Phone Number: _____ Email: _____
Account Balance: _____ Date of Balance: _____

Name of Lender: _____
Address of Real Estate: _____
Loan Number: _____
Phone Number: _____ Email: _____
Account Balance: _____ Date of Balance: _____

Name of Lender: _____
Address of Real Estate: _____
Loan Number: _____
Phone Number: _____ Email: _____
Account Balance: _____ Date of Balance: _____

Name of Lender: _____
Address of Real Estate: _____
Loan Number: _____
Phone Number: _____ Email: _____
Account Balance: _____ Date of Balance: _____

Cars, Boats and Motorcycle Loans:

Name of Lender: _____
Type and Description of Vehicle: _____
Loan Number: _____
Phone Number: _____ Email: _____
Account Balance: _____ Date of Balance: _____

CULTURAL ARCHITECTS

Name of Lender: _____
Type and Description of Vehicle: _____
Loan Number: _____
Phone Number: _____ Email: _____
Account Balance: _____ Date of Balance: _____

Name of Lender: _____
Type and Description of Vehicle: _____
Loan Number: _____
Phone Number: _____ Email: _____
Account Balance: _____ Date of Balance: _____

Name of Lender: _____
Type and Description of Vehicle: _____
Loan Number: _____
Phone Number: _____ Email: _____
Account Balance: _____ Date of Balance: _____

Name of Lender: _____
Type and Description of Vehicle: _____
Loan Number: _____
Phone Number: _____ Email: _____
Account Balance: _____ Date of Balance: _____

General Consumer Credit Loans:

Name of Lender: _____
Loan Number: _____
Phone Number: _____ Email: _____
Account Balance: _____ Date of Balance: _____

Name of Lender: _____
Loan Number: _____
Phone Number: _____ Email: _____
Account Balance: _____ Date of Balance: _____

Name of Lender: _____
Loan Number: _____
Phone Number: _____ Email: _____
Account Balance: _____ Date of Balance: _____

Name of Lender: _____
Loan Number: _____
Phone Number: _____ Email: _____
Account Balance: _____ Date of Balance: _____

CULTURAL ARCHITECTS

Personal Loans Made to You:

Person Who Made Loan: _____
Phone Number: _____ Email: _____
Loan Balance: _____ Date of Balance: _____

Person Who Made Loan: _____
Phone Number: _____ Email: _____
Loan Balance: _____ Date of Balance: _____

Person Who Made Loan: _____
Phone Number: _____ Email: _____
Loan Balance: _____ Date of Balance: _____

Person Who Made Loan: _____
Phone Number: _____ Email: _____
Loan Balance: _____ Date of Balance: _____

Personal Loans You Have Made to Others:

Name of Borrower: _____
Phone Number: _____ Email: _____
Loan Balance: _____
Purpose of Loan: _____
Loan Balance: _____ Date of Balance: _____

Name of Borrower: _____
Phone Number: _____ Email: _____
Loan Balance: _____
Purpose of Loan: _____
Loan Balance: _____ Date of Balance: _____

Name of Borrower: _____
Phone Number: _____ Email: _____
Loan Balance: _____
Purpose of Loan: _____
Loan Balance: _____ Date of Balance: _____

Name of Borrower:
_____ Phone Number:
_____ Email: _____ Loan Balance
_____ Purpose of
Loan: _____ Loan
Balance: _____ Date of Balance: _____

CULTURAL ARCHITECTS

FAMILY LEGACY IMPARTATION PROTOCOL

Family Legacy-
Unfinished Business Form No. 5

THE FAMILY
REFORMATION PROJECT

LIST OF ALL CREDIT CARD ACCOUNTS

Your heirs or executor will need this information to immediately close the accounts to protect your estate from identity theft as well as to arrange for payments of all outstanding balances.

Name of Credit Card:_____
Account Number: _____ Phone Number: _____
Account Balance: _____ Date of Balance: _____
List All Automatic Payments, On-Line, PayPal and Other Accounts That Use This Card:
_____
_____
_____

Name of Credit Card:_____
Account Number: _____ Phone Number: _____
Account Balance: _____ Date of Balance: _____
List All Automatic Payments, On-Line, PayPal and Other Accounts That Use This Card:
_____
_____
_____

Name of Credit Card:_____
Account Number: _____ Phone Number: _____
Account Balance: _____ Date of Balance: _____
List All Automatic Payments, On-Line, PayPal and Other Accounts That Use This Card:
_____
_____
_____

Name of Credit Card:_____
Account Number: _____ Phone Number: _____
Account Balance: _____ Date of Balance: _____
List All Automatic Payments, On-Line, PayPal and Other Accounts That Use This Card:
_____
_____
_____

CULTURAL ARCHITECTS

Name of Credit Card:_____
Account Number: _____ Phone Number: _____
Account Balance: _____ Date of Balance: _____
List All Automatic Payments, On-Line, PayPal and Other Accounts That Use This Card:
_____
_____
_____

Name of Credit Card:_____
Account Number: _____ Phone Number: _____
Account Balance: _____ Date of Balance: _____
List All Automatic Payments, On-Line, PayPal and Other Accounts That Use This Card:
_____
_____
_____

Name of Credit Card:_____
Account Number: _____ Phone Number: _____
Account Balance: _____ Date of Balance: _____
List All Automatic Payments, On-Line, PayPal and Other Accounts That Use This Card:
_____
_____
_____

Name of Credit Card:_____
Account Number: _____ Phone Number: _____
Account Balance: _____ Date of Balance: _____
List All Automatic Payments, On-Line, PayPal and Other Accounts That Use This Card:
_____
_____
_____

Total Outstanding Credit Card Debt and Date of Balance: _____

CULTURAL ARCHITECTS

FAMILY LEGACY IMPARTATION PROTOCOL

Family Legacy-
Unfinished Business Form No. 6

THE FAMILY
REFORMATION PROJECT

DETAILED CHILD CARE INSTRUCTIONS

Child One:

Name of Child: _____ Date of Birth _____

Significant Medical Condition(s):

[ ]

Ongoing Care Requirements for Significant Medical Condition:

[ ]

Food Allergies:

[ ]

Special Dietary Considerations, Medications and Dosages:

[ ]

Name of Primary Doctor: _____ Phone # _____

Names and Phone Numbers of Regular Babysitters:

[ ]

CULTURAL ARCHITECTS

Name and Phone Number of School or Daycare Being Attended:

```
[                                                                    ]
```

School Transportation (How to get to school, time and place to meet bus, carpool, etc.):

```
[                                                                    ]
```

List of Tutoring, Special Needs, or Other Non-School Activities:

```
[                                                                    ]
```

List of Child's Sports, Scouting, and Other Extracurricular Activities:

Activity: _____
When & Where: _____
Time(s): _____
Contact Name & No.: _____

Activity: _____
When & Where: _____
Time(s): _____
Contact Name & No.: _____

Activity: _____
When & Where: _____
Time(s): _____
Contact Name & No.: _____

Activity: _____
When & Where: _____
Time(s): _____
Contact Name & No.: _____

Bed Time, Nap Time(s) & Wake-up Time in Morning:

```
[                                                                    ]
```

CULTURAL ARCHITECTS

Any Special Instructions:

[ ]

Child Two:

Name of Child: _____ Date of Birth _____

Significant Medical Condition(s):

[ ]

Ongoing Care Requirements for Significant Medical Condition:

[ ]

Food Allergies:

[ ]

Special Dietary Considerations, Medications and Dosages:

[ ]

Name of Primary Doctor: _____ Phone # _____

Names and Phone Numbers of Regular Babysitters

[ ]

CULTURAL ARCHITECTS

Name and Phone Number of School or Daycare Being Attended:

```
┌─────────────────────────────────────────────────────────┐
│                                                           │
│                                                           │
│                                                           │
└─────────────────────────────────────────────────────────┘
```

School Transportation (How to get to school, time and place to meet bus, carpool, etc.):

```
┌─────────────────────────────────────────────────────────┐
│                                                           │
│                                                           │
│                                                           │
└─────────────────────────────────────────────────────────┘
```

List of Tutoring, Special Needs, or Other Non-School Activities:

```
┌─────────────────────────────────────────────────────────┐
│                                                           │
│                                                           │
│                                                           │
└─────────────────────────────────────────────────────────┘
```

List of Child's Sports, Scouting, and Other Extracurricular Activities:

Activity: _____
When & Where: _____
Time(s): _____
Contact Name & No.: _____

Activity: _____
When & Where: _____
Time(s): _____
Contact Name & No.: _____

Activity: _____
When & Where: _____
Time(s): _____
Contact Name & No.: _____

Activity: _____
When & Where: _____
Time(s): _____
Contact Name & No.: _____

Bed Time, Nap Time(s) & Wake-up Time in Morning:

```
┌─────────────────────────────────────────────────────────┐
│                                                           │
│                                                           │
│                                                           │
└─────────────────────────────────────────────────────────┘
```

CULTURAL ARCHITECTS

Any Special Instructions:

[ ]

Child Three:

Name of Child: _____ Date of Birth _____

Significant Medical Condition(s):

[ ]

Ongoing Care Requirements for Significant Medical Condition:

[ ]

Food Allergies:

[ ]

Special Dietary Considerations, Medications and Dosages:

[ ]

Name of Primary Doctor: _____ Phone # _____

Names and Phone Numbers of Regular Babysitters:

[ ]

CULTURAL ARCHITECTS

Name and Phone Number of School or Daycare Being Attended:

```
┌──────────────────────────────────────────────────────────┐
│                                                            │
│                                                            │
│                                                            │
└──────────────────────────────────────────────────────────┘
```

School Transportation (How to get to school, time and place to meet bus, carpool, etc.):

```
┌──────────────────────────────────────────────────────────┐
│                                                            │
│                                                            │
│                                                            │
└──────────────────────────────────────────────────────────┘
```

List of Tutoring, Special Needs, or Other Non-School Activities:

```
┌──────────────────────────────────────────────────────────┐
│                                                            │
│                                                            │
└──────────────────────────────────────────────────────────┘
```

List of Child's Sports, Scouting, and Other Extracurricular Activities:

Activity: _____
When & Where: _____
Time(s): _____
Contact Name & No.: _____

Activity: _____
When & Where: _____
Time(s): _____
Contact Name & No.: _____

Activity: _____
When & Where: _____
Time(s): _____
Contact Name & No.: _____

Activity: _____
When & Where: _____
Time(s): _____
Contact Name & No.: _____

Bed Time, Nap Time(s) & Wake-up Time in Morning:

```
┌──────────────────────────────────────────────────────────┐
│                                                            │
│                                                            │
│                                                            │
└──────────────────────────────────────────────────────────┘
```

CULTURAL ARCHITECTS

Any Special Instructions:

CULTURAL ARCHITECTS

THE FAMILY
REFORMATION PROJECT

FAMILY LEGACY IMPARTATION PROTOCOL

Family Legacy-
Unfinished Business Form No. 7

Home Utility and Service Providers:

PERMISSION TO SHARE INFORMATION REGARDING MISCELLANEOUS PERSONAL/HOUSEHOLD MATTERS WITH OTHERS

_____ has my permission to contact any of the individuals or companies listed below and for them to undertake any of the matters selected under the circumstances specified. I have placed my initials next to those matters that are being included with this Permission:

___ **Utility Companies**:
Phone and Account No. of Electric Company:_____
Phone and Account No. of Gas Company: _____
Phone and Account No. of Water Company: _____
Phone and Account No. of Septic/Sewage: _____
Phone and Account No. of Telephone Company: _____
Phone and Account No. of Cell Phone Company: _____
Phone and Account No. of Satellite, Cable or other Television Company:

_____

___ **Internet Provider:** Please provide the above-named individual with all information in connection with my account and permit them to undertake all of the following matters next to my initials:

___ **Miscellaneous Household Services:** Please provide the above-named individual with all information in connection with the following listed services and permit them to undertake all actions that are indicated next to my initials:

Trash Removal:

Name of Company: _____
Telephone Number: _____
Which Days Collected: _____
Location of Pick Up: _____

CULTURAL /\RCHITECTS

House Cleaning:

Name of Company or Individual: _____
Telephone Number:_____

Cleaning Schedule: _____
Services Provided: _____

Lawn Cutting & Related Services:

Name of Company or Individual:_____
Telephone Number: _____
Services Provided: _____

Snow Removal Services:

Name of Company or Individual:_____
Telephone Number: _____
Services Provided: _____

List any additional services to be included along with needed information.

```



```

Please provide the above-named individual with any and all information in connection with my account as well as services being provided and to permit them to undertake any of the following matters next to my initials:

____ Cancel my service(s and close my account
____ Request repairs
____ Request additional, reduced, or changed services
____ Dispute, pay or negotiate payment of my account balances

This Permission is being given on the ____ day of _____, _____.

_____ Signature of Person Giving Permission

_____ Printed Name of Person Giving Permission

CULTURAL ARCHITECTS

THE FAMILY
REFORMATION PROJECT

FAMILY LEGACY IMPARTATION PROTOCOL

Family Legacy-
Unfinished Business Form No. 8

Ownership of Pet(s) Upon Death:

Make certain that your pet(s) have a good home when you die by designating in writing who will be undertaking their care upon your death.

In the event of my death, I _____ hereby direct that my pet(s) shall go to the following person(s) to be cared for by them and become their property, as follows:

Pet One:

Name, Description and Type of Pet:

```


```

Name, Phone Number and Address of Person to Take this Pet:

```


```

Pet Two:

Name, Description and Type of Pet:

```


```

Name, Phone Number and Address of Person to Take this Pet:

```


```

CULTURAL /\RCHITECTS

FAMILY LEGACY IMPARTATION PROTOCOL

Family Legacy-
Unfinished Business Form No. 9

THE FAMILY
REFORMATION PROJECT

Pet Care Instructions:

If someone is going to care for your pet(s) for some period of time, whether because of a planned absence or in an emergency, it's important that those caring for them are aware of any information that could affect their well-being.

Pet One:

Type of Pet: _____

Year Pet was Born: _____

Description of Pet: _____

Is Pet Friendly to Non-Family Members: _____

Is Your Pet Allowed Out of Doors Without Supervision ☐ Yes ☐ No

Is Your Pet Allowed Out of Doors With Supervision ☐ Yes ☐ No

If Your Pet is a Cat and Declawed: ☐ Yes ☐ No

Name, Address and Phone Number of Pet's Veterinarian

| |
| |

List Any On-Going Medical Conditions That Require Treatment and Describe the Treatment (example: diabetes, heart worm, allergies, fleas, etc.):

| |
| |

List all prior surgeries and other past, serious medical treatments:

| |
| |

Describe Any Unusual Behavior Issues (example: Is your pet unusually afraid of storms, does it become aggressive or upset if picked up or touched in a certain part of its body, is it sensitive to excessive heat, etc.):

| |
| |

List Any Additional, Important Information About This Pet:

Pet Two:

Type of Pet: _____

Year Pet was Born: _____

Description of Pet: _____

Is Pet Friendly to Non-Family Members: _____

Is Your Pet Allowed Out of Doors Without Supervision ☐ Yes ☐ No

Is Your Pet Allowed Out of Doors With Supervision ☐ Yes ☐ No

If Your Pet is a Cat and Declawed: ☐ Yes ☐ No

Name, Address and Phone Number of Pet's Veterinarian

List Any On-Going Medical Conditions That Require Treatment and Describe the Treatment (example: diabetes, heart worm, allergies, fleas, etc.):

List all prior surgeries and other past, serious medical treatments:

Describe Any Unusual Behavior Issues (example: Is your pet unusually afraid of storms, does it become aggressive or upset if picked up or touched in a certain part of its body, is it sensitive to excessive heat, etc.):

List Any Additional, Important Information About This Pet:

CULTURAL ARCHITECTS

FAMILY LEGACY IMPARTATION PROTOCOL

Family Legacy-
Unfinished Business Form No. 10

THE FAMILY
REFORMATION PROJECT

LIST OF ALL INSURANCE POLICIES

Life Insurance:

Name of Insurance Company: _____
Contact Person at Company (if any: _____
Company Phone No. and/or E-Mail Address: _____
Policy Number: _____
Policy Amount: _____
Access Code/Password (if any: _____

Name of Insurance Company: _____
Contact Person at Company (if any: _____
Company Phone No. and/or E-Mail Address: _____
Policy Number: _____
Policy Amount: _____
Access Code/Password (if any: _____

Name of Insurance Company: _____
Contact Person at Company (if any: _____
Company Phone No. and/or E-Mail Address: _____
Policy Number: _____
Policy Amount: _____
Access Code/Password (if any: _____

Name of Insurance Company: _____
Contact Person at Company (if any: _____
Company Phone No. and/or E-Mail Address: _____
Policy Number: _____
Policy Amount: _____
Access Code/Password (if any: _____

Home Owners Insurance:

Name of Insurance Company: _____
Contact Person at Company (if any: _____
Company Phone No. and/or E-Mail Address: _____

CULTURAL ARCHITECTS

Policy Number: _____
Policy Amount: _____
Access Code/Password (if any: _____
Name of Insurance Company: _____
Contact Person at Company (if any: _____
Company Phone No. and/or E-Mail Address: _____
Policy Number: _____
Policy Amount: _____
Access Code/Password (if any: _____

Rental Insurance:

Name of Insurance Company: _____
Contact Person at Company (if any: _____
Company Phone No. and/or E-Mail Address: _____
Policy Number: _____
Policy Amount: _____
Access Code/Password (if any: _____

Disability Insurance:

Name of Insurance Company: _____
Contact Person at Company (if any: _____
Company Phone No. and/or E-Mail Address: _____
Policy Number: _____
Policy Amount: _____
Access Code/Password (if any: _____

Medical Insurance:

Name of Insurance Company: _____
Contact Person at Company (if any: _____
Company Phone No. and/or E-Mail Address: _____
Policy Number: _____
Policy Amount: _____
Access Code/Password (if any: _____

Automobile Insurance:

Name of Insurance Company: _____
Contact Person at Company (if any: _____
Company Phone No. and/or E-Mail Address: _____
Policy Number: _____
Policy Amount: _____
Access Code/Password (if any): _____

CULTURAL ARCHITECTS

Name of Insurance Company: _____
Contact Person at Company (if any: _____
Company Phone No. and/or E-Mail Address: _____
Policy Number: _____
Policy Amount: _____
Access Code/Password (if any: _____

Umbrella / Liability Insurance

Name of Insurance Company: _____
Contact Person at Company (if any: _____
Company Phone No. and/or E-Mail Address: _____
Policy Number: _____
Policy Amount: _____
Access Code/Password (if any: _____

Name of Insurance Company: _____
Contact Person at Company (if any: _____
Company Phone No. and/or E-Mail Address: _____
Policy Number: _____
Policy Amount: _____
Access Code/Password (if any: _____

Miscellaneous Insurance:

Type of Insurance: _____
Name of Insurance Company: _____
Contact Person at Company (if any: _____
Company Phone No. and/or E-Mail Address: _____
Policy Number: _____
Policy Amount: _____
Access Code/Password (if any): _____

CULTURAL ARCHITECTS

THE FAMILY
REFORMATION PROJECT

FAMILY LEGACY IMPARTATION PROTOCOL

Family Legacy-
The Unfinished Business Form No. 11

LIST OF ALL BUSINESS BANK ACCOUNTS

Name of Bank or Credit Union: _____
Account Number: _____
Any Access Code/Password: _____
Web address for online Banking: _____
Account Balance and Date of Balance: _____

Name of Bank or Credit Union: _____
Account Number: _____
Any Access Code/Password: _____
Web address for online Banking: _____
Account Balance and Date of Balance: _____

Name of Bank or Credit Union: _____
Account Number: _____
Any Access Code/Password: _____
Web address for online Banking: _____
Account Balance and Date of Balance: _____

Name of Bank or Credit Union: _____
Account Number: _____
Any Access Code/Password: _____
Web address for online Banking: _____
Account Balance and Date of Balance: _____

Name of Bank or Credit Union: _____
Account Number: _____
Any Access Code/Password: _____
Web address for online Banking: _____
Account Balance and Date of Balance: _____

Location of checkbook, checks and statements:

[   ]

CULTURAL ARCHITECTS

THE FAMILY
REFORMATION PROJECT

FAMILY LEGACY IMPARTATION PROTOCOL

Family Legacy-
the Unfinished Business Form No. 12

LIST OF BUSINESS LOANS, CREDIT CARDS & OTHER DEBTS

Loans:

Name of Lender: _____
Loan Number: _____
Contact Person: _____
Phone Number: _____

Name of Lender: _____
Loan Number: _____
Contact Person: _____
Phone Number: _____

Name of Lender: _____
Loan Number: _____
Contact Person: _____
Phone Number: _____

Name of Lender: _____
Loan Number: _____
Contact Person: _____
Phone Number: _____

Credit Cards:

Card Name:_____
Account Number: _____
Website/Password:_____
Phone Number: _____

Card Name:_____
Account Number: _____
Website/Password:_____
Phone Number: _____

CULTURAL ARCHITECTS

Card Name:_____
Account Number: _____
Website/Password:_____
Phone Number: _____

Card Name:_____
Account Number: _____
Website/Password:_____
Phone Number: _____

LIST OF BUSINESS LOANS, CREDIT CARDS & OTHER DEBTS

Vehicle, Office Equipment, Office and Other Leases:

Type of Lease: _____
Name of Company: _____
Lease Number: _____
Phone number: _____
Website / Password _____

Type of Lease: _____
Name of Company: _____
Lease Number: _____
Phone number: _____
Website / Password _____

Miscellaneous Loans and Debts: (provide source of debt, contact person and phone number):

Location of Loan Documents and Other Paper Work:

List of Book Keepers, Accountants, and Any Other Individuals or Companies that May Have Detailed Information Regarding Your Business' Financial Information: (Include Phone Numbers, E-Mail Addresses, and Any Other Contact Information):

CULTURAL ARCHITECTS

FAMILY LEGACY IMPARTATION PROTOCOL

Family Legacy-
Unfinished Business Form No. 13

THE FAMILY
REFORMATION PROJECT

BUSINESS DIGITAL FOOTPRINT INFORMATION

COMPUTER, EMAIL, CELLPHONE, ACCOUNTS AND OTHER PASSWORDS

Office 1:
Address: _____
Security Code: _____
Garage Keypad Code: _____
Location of Keys: _____

Office 2:
Address: _____
Security Code: _____
Garage Keypad Code: _____
Location of Keys: _____

Business Phone Numbers and Passwords:
Phone number: _____
Username/Password_____

Phone number: _____
Username/Password_____

Phone number: _____
Username/Password_____

Business Email Addresses and Passwords:
Email Address: _____
Username/Password_____

Email Address: _____
Username/Password_____

Email Address: _____
Username/Password_____

Email Address:_____
Username/Password_____

CULTURAL ARCHITECTS

Business Wi Fi Network
Name of home Wi-Fi network: _____
Username / Password _____

Business Computer Passwords:
Description and location of computer(s
Computer: _____
Username/Password: _____

Description and location of computer(s
Computer: _____
Username/Password: _____

Description and location of computer(s
Computer: _____
Username/Password: _____

Description and location of computer(s
Computer: _____
Username/Password: _____

Business On-line Apps and Accounts:
(Amazon, eBay, Facebook, Instagram, Expedia, Delta, etc.

Web Address: _____
Username/Password: _____

Web Address: _____
Username/Password: _____

Web Address: _____
Username/Password: _____

Web Address: _____
Username/Password: _____

Web Address: _____
Username/Password: _____

Web Address: _____
Username/Password: _____

CULTURAL ARCHITECTS

List all other passwords and access codes: (storage, gate access, padlocks, briefcases)

CULTURAL ARCHITECTS

FAMILY LEGACY IMPARTATION PROTOCOL

Family Legacy-
Unfinished Business Form No. 14

THE FAMILY
REFORMATION PROJECT

Work/Business Notification List:

Name of Person:_____
Business or Affiliation: _____
Phone Number: _____
E-mail Address: _____

Name of Person:_____
Business or Affiliation: _____
Phone Number: _____
E-mail Address: _____

Name of Person:_____
Business or Affiliation: _____
Phone Number: _____
E-mail Address: _____

Name of Person:_____
Business or Affiliation: _____
Phone Number: _____
E-mail Address: _____

Name of Person:_____
Business or Affiliation: _____
Phone Number: _____
E-mail Address: _____

Name of Person:_____
Business or Affiliation: _____
Phone Number: _____
E-mail Address: _____

Name of Person:_____
Business or Affiliation: _____
Phone Number: _____
E-mail Address: _____

THE FAMILY
REFORMATION PROJECT

FAMILY LEGACY IMPARTATION PROTOCOL

Family Legacy-
Generational Covenant Tool™

The final piece of the Family Legacy Impartation Protocol is the Family Legacy Generational Covenant. This covenant is an intentional conveying upon the next generation the responsibility of stewarding the family legacy faithfully in their lifetime. It is also a practice designed to be repeated with each generation to ensure this stewardship of legacy endures.

A covenant is the highest form of agreement between two or more parties, based on the biblical example and definition. God made a covenant with Abraham that was transferred to Isaac, then to Jacob, and so on. We have the old and new covenants in the scriptures. An agreement between God Himself and man. A covenant is a sacred promise or agreement that all parties who choose to be involved will do what they have agreed to do for generations. It is an all-in, whatever it takes, no turning back, and no giving up agreement between parties. Biblically, covenants were sealed with the shedding of blood; or in other words, "On the promise of my life, I will keep this covenant, and so will my entire house (family."

God's idea of covenant is sobering, life-giving, and powerful. The Family Legacy Generational Covenant is patterned after the same idea of making a sacred promise to do what all parties are agreeing to do with the intensity of an all-in, whatever-it-takes commitment that includes the generations to come. It is a deep and sober commitment from the heart to build and steward the family legacy faithfully and for the purposes and glory of God. The Family Legacy Generational Covenant exercise is simply the completion and execution of the tool.

Explanation
When God wanted His chosen family to remember something important, He attached an action or a practice to it to create a trigger that reminded them of the significance of that thing. God instituted various ceremonies, festivals, feasts, holy days, symbols, practices, sacraments, ordinances, and protocols so that the meaning underneath these containers could be conveyed to everyone and passed on from generation to generation as His legacy.

Communion, baptism, Passover, and the bar mitzvah are all examples of ways that God formalized important spiritual truths and practices into containers that could be duplicated and passed on for generations in a way that could be understood and continued.

This is what the Family Legacy Generational Covenant is about. It is an intentional practice of formally making a lasting covenant between parent(s, their children, and God to ensure the stewardship of the family legacy in perpetuity for the glory of God. No one is compelled to make this covenant. Family members have the opportunity to choose in.

Before you are tempted to minimize the power of agreement, consider that God has chosen to govern all creation, to relate to humankind, even to put our inheritance along with His own credibility all in the framework of agreements and covenants. Making an agreement is a big deal.

The Family Legacy Generational Covenant Tool

The Family Legacy Generational Covenant is also a covenant between families. It is an agreement between your family and God, who by very nature is a family (Father, Son, Holy Spirit. It is a sacred choice to faithfully steward your family identity, purpose, values, and sovereign design. It is an agreement entered into by choice and made with everyone else in the family who is choosing "in" to this responsibility with you.

The Ceremony

The purpose of the ceremony is to emphasize the importance of faithfully stewarding the family legacy while gaining the commitment and agreement of the next generation to continue in the protocols and to do the same with their children.

The Family Legacy Generational Covenant ceremony should take place face-to-face with the entire family once the family has been introduced to the protocols contained in the Family Legacy Model. It may be especially impactful when it is time for the ones who have been carrying the main responsibility for the legacy work to pass that primary responsibility on to someone else. End of life would be one good time for the ceremony. Another effective time to hold the ceremony is at the end of the Family Legacy Encounter Workshop where we spend the better part of three days with a single family, walking them through all the protocols. By the time the family has engaged in the learning experience and knows how to execute the protocols, a family covenant before God to prioritize and carry out the protocols faithfully is a powerful culmination of the encounter.
It may also be a good idea to record on video the ceremony as a leader and keep with the other legacy content for use in the event of unexpected death.

Instructions
Leader:
Gather the family in a semicircle with the parent(s standing out in front of the family facing them. Determine which parent will lead the covenant.

Leader:
"God in Heaven, we the __(Last name)___ family have gathered before you to make a sacred covenant with each other and with You (Father, Son, and Holy Spirit).
"Whereas, by Your good, wise, and eternal design, You have set us in this family from before the foundations of the world, and
"Whereas, Your design for our family line is to bring glory and honor to Your great name and to advance Your eternal kingdom by shaping culture from the inside out, and
"Whereas, You have bestowed upon our family line Your character, Your love, Your purposes, and Your power to accomplish this in agreement with Your design, and

(Continued next page)

The Family Legacy Generational Covenant Tool   (Continued)

"Whereas, You have made known to us the design for how to live and leave a powerful and enduring family legacy in Your Word, and
"Whereas, the Family Legacy Protocols are patterned after and in full agreement with Your design,
"All who are willing to join in this decree, repeat after me."
"I choose to be a wise builder." (Repeat.
"I commit to building our family, our businesses, our community, and our culture." (Repeat.
"And through intelligence and insight," (repeat
"Together as one with You and this family," (repeat
"Our enterprises are established and endure" (repeat
"For the glory of our King and His kingdom." (repeat
"So be it!" (Repeat.

Leader:
"Knowing that You are a good Father and that You keep Your covenants to always do Your part in ensuring that Your legacy is fulfilled in our family line, we now offer our agreements in our Family Legacy Generational Covenant with You.

"All who are willing to join in this covenant, repeat after me."
"I commit to wholeheartedly engage in the faithful stewardship of my family legacy regularly." (Repeat.
"I agree to give my best effort to practice the Family Legacy Protocols personally," (repeat
"with my family of origin" (repeat
"and with my own children." (repeat
"I agree to reach out for help and support in keeping this covenant when challenged." (Repeat.
"I commit to equipping my children and grandchildren to use the Family Legacy Protocols," (repeat
"and to instruct them to do the same." (repeat
"I choose to live and leave a powerful and enduring family legacy to the glory of God." (Repeat.
"I commit to help other families understand and use the protocols as God directs me." (Repeat.

Leader:
A closing prayer from the heart would be appropriate here.

Made in United States
North Haven, CT
09 June 2023